PRAYING SCRIPTURES

I DECREE AND DECLARE VOL. 1b

WALE-RICH OLADUNJOYE

GREATMINDS PRIME CREST PUBLISHERS LTD

Copyright © 2021 WALE-RICH OLADUNJOYE

All rights reserved

No part of this book may be reproduced, or stored in a retrieval system, or transmitted in any form or by any means, electronic, mechanical, photocopying, recording, or otherwise, without express written permission of the publisher.

ISBN- 9798501223721

INTRODUCTION

The BOOK PRAYING SCRIPTURES (PS) is considered by many to be one of the priceless possessions of everyone, ranking alongside the first ever best printed daily prayer book.

It has been said with some justice that the words of this Prayer Book have been prayed and recited by people of different nations far more frequently than you may think before putting it to writing.

I first started in 2016 by praying individually for different people in the night season before the prayer requests became longer than the available time. Then I began to send prayers to people via short messages service (SMS) and WhatsApp.

The contents of this book have been utilised by Christians and non- Christians throughout the world, having many of its phrases becoming part of our everday languageand still influencing the worship and devotions of millions of both Christians and non- Christians today.

The PRAYING SCRIPTURES comes to us in a number of volumes and is usually referred to as "I DECREE AND DECLARE".

The first book covers a year and divided into four parts Vol.1a, Vol.1b, Vol.1c, Vol 1d, each one covering each quaters.

In essence , the PRAYING SCRIPTURE BOOK is written and released in series. Each of the four series covering a year, features a common layout and are related to each other however the content of each series shows a considerble coverage of different needs and demands. In a sense the PRAYING SCRIPTURES can be looked on as a wonderful example of a book which contains a whole range of what every individual needs for divine intervention.

Your personal copy is a must.

PRAYING SCRIPTURES
[I DECREE & DECLARE]
Vol. 1b

PRAYING SCRIPTURES VOLUME 1b COVERS THE NEXT 90-181 DAYS OF THE YEAR.

PRAYING SCRIPTURES

[I DECREE & DECLARE]

This All-Seasons Daily Praying Scriptures

Is Presented to

On This Day

By

Praying Scriptures Daily helps and Guides for Every Day Victory in Every Aspect of Life

Volume 1, No 1b

Copyright 2021

WALE-RICH OLADUNJOYE

ISBN: 9798501223721

E-mail: pastorwale2001@yahoo.com

walerichman@gmail.com;

Facebook: wale.oladunjoye.7@facebook.com

Twitter: walerich_62

Skype: walerich6

Publishers: Great Minds Prime Crest Ltd;

Telephone number: 08035779346

TABLE OF CONTENT

TITLE PAGE

COPY RIGHT/DEDICATION

ACKNOWELDGEMENT/ INTRODUCTION

MY MOTIVATION

MY PURPOSE FOR WRITING THIS BOOK

HOW TO USE THIS PRAYER BOOK

FIRST THINGS FIRST [YOU MUST BE BORN AGAIN]

PRAYERS FOR EACH DAY- APRIL

PRAYERS FOR EACH DAY-MAY

PRAYERS FOR EACH DAY-JUNE

BOOKS BY THE AUTHOR/ABOUT THE AUTHOR

ACKNOWELDGEMENT

I am glad at this moment to acknowledge my parents who brought me up in the ways of the Lord. I saw my father as a child daily waking up praying from 4am till 6am before heading to the church for devotion. He was a great intercessor!

I acknowledge my wife who has been encouraging me to do more and providing the enabling environment for good work to be done.

I acknowledge my children who are also progressively learning about the kingdom of God with their full strength.

My acknoweldgement goes to everyone who participated and donated towards the (KED) Kingdom Expansion Donations.

I will also like to acknoweldge my book editors John Oladunjoye and Rosemary Mgbeze who doggedly worked

both day and night to meet the standard and schedule of the book.   Thank you all

MY MOTIVATION

2 Timothy 2:1-2

"Thou therefore, my son, be strong in the grace that is in Christ Jesus. And the things that thou hast heard of me among many witnesses, the same commit thou to faithful men, who shall be able to teach others also."

One of the things among many that I watched my father did was his prayer life. I saw him consistently daily waking up in the night time and especially by 4 a.m. praying all manners of prayers which included praying for each of his children and interceding for as many people as came to his mind.

I watched him praying until something would happen. I saw him praying for the sick, for the pregnant women finding delivery of babies difficult, praying for the dead until they came back to life. In a nut shell, our family house was a house of prayers.

From this experience, I grew up to know the importance and power of prayers. I grew up developing or having faith that my prayers in the name of Jesus Christ can move the mountains.

I discovered there is power in my tongue.

Proverbs 18:21

"Death and life are in the power of the tongue: and they that love it shall eat the fruit thereof." I therefore, started praying for as many people as needed prayers. Whenever I sensed the battle was tough, I usually shift the battle to the night season especially between 12 midnight and 3 a.m.

Before you say Jack Robinson, the queue of the people waiting to be prayed for became too long to be handled within the available time in the night season.

Then the Holy Ghost taught me to send the prayers to everyone via electronic media. This method paid off, it was a huge relieve and widened the coverage of my prayers.

As at this point of converting these powerful prayers to book,

56 countries were already affected positively, this includes the countries termed as non-Christian catchment areas.

Converting these prayers to book form became a necessity based on people's demand and for the facts that sometimes the electronic transmission fails.

Having gotten this far, I like to say glory to God and congratulations to all the users.

MY PURPOSE FOR WRITING THIS BOOK

To me, Prayer is my breath, my food, my method of maintaining my spiritual well being and service to humanity.

What I enjoy most is interceding for others; repairing emotional wounds, offering spiritual intervention to people where necessary and meeting the public needs.

I wrote the series of this book and am still writing because it's an act of obedience to God. We are called to pray.

God designed us for it. It's built into our very existence.

This is because we are created in His image-God's image, we are to display Christ-like behaviour. Jesus prayed to remain in the Father's will. So as Christ imitators prayer is necessary to remain in His will also.

FOR PERSONAL PRAYER

Jesus prayed personally; "Before daybreak the next morning, Jesus got up and went out to an isolated place to pray (Mark 1:35)

FOR INTERCESSION

Jesus prayed for others; "My prayer is not for the world, but for those you have given me, because they belong to you (John 17:1)

FOR CONGREGATIONAL PRAYERS

The disciples prayed together, "They all met together and were constantly united in prayer, along with Mary, the mother of Jesus, several other women, and the brothers of Jesus (Acts 1:4)

This prayer book is important because prayer is the solution. Prayer is an avenue to resolution, the path to finding an answer to a problem. It provides insight to our dilemmas and tough decisions.

Ask me, this book will offer you remarkable secrets you need to know about answered prayers.

HOW TO USE THIS DAILY PRAYING SCRIPTURES

This Praying Scriptures book is to make prayer life enjoyable for you. Scriptures are picked to address various issue of life. It addresses specific issues that may be affecting you and your family and with the intention of providing solutions to them. There is no doubt, if you consistently use this prayer book, you will eventually know how to pray fervently and effectually.

There is always a scripture or more quoted and followed by thanksgiving then to decrees and declarations.

Job 22:28 *Thou shalt also decree a thing, and it shall be established unto thee: and the light shall shine upon thy ways.*

The prayers are done in a highly personalized manner that makes things happen instantly and eventually.

James 5:16-18 says that, "...The effectual fervent prayer of a righteous man availeth much.

Elias was a man subject to like passions as we are, and he prayed earnestly that it might not rain: and it rained not on the earth by the space of three years and six months.

And he prayed again, and the heaven gave rain, and the earth brought forth her fruit."

The prayers here are scriptural based that when you pray them fervently you make things happen as occasion demands.

Remember, *Isaiah 55:10-11 says, "For as the rain cometh down, and the snow from heaven, and returneth not thither, but watereth the earth, and maketh it bring forth and bud, that it may give seed to the sower, and bread to the eater:*

So shall my word be that goeth forth out of my mouth: it shall not return unto me void, but it shall accomplish that which I please, and it shall prosper in the thing whereto I sent it."

This prayer manual is designed to be used both FOR and AGAINST.

The prayers are strong enough to bring you favor, peace, prosperity, breakthrough, victory, healing, success and etcetera and powerful enough to bring down the head of Goliaths, Pharaohs, haters and satanic agents around you.

They are potent to destroy yokes and forcefully lift demonic embargoes.

People use them to break barriers to marital chaos and stagnations.

When used, deliverance happens in the name of the Lord.

When you engage in this kind of prayers you become unharassable, untouchable, unmolestable, unconquerable, unpunishable by the enemies, unkillable and unbeatable.

This is an all-purpose prayer book for all seasons and in all situations.

You can scan through or follow it day-by-day.

Just use as occasion demands and answers to your prayers are guaranteed by the grace of God.

Daily Praying Scriptures Has Resolved tough matters and situations.

It Has Dissolved issues and Reshaped Beaten and Battered Destinies.

It Has Generated Miracles and Testimonies in a Higher Frequency than Humanly Expected.

Currently as of The Time of This Publication, Praying Scriptures Has Gone Viral in Many Countries and Nations of The World. The Praying Scripture Is Being Accepted and Put to Use Both Online and Offline in About Fifty-Six (56) Countries.

The Amazing Thing is That Praying Scriptures is Still Passing from One Hand to Another and From One Household to Another Doing Wonders and Giving Answers to Seemingly Impossible Cases Through the Grace Made Available by God.

The Prayers are Anointed for Performance

Enjoy your prayer life and recommend this for your friends and loved ones.

And remember to share your testimonies with us because you shall certainly have them after your prayers.

I wish you the best and God's favour.

FIRST THING FIRST (YOU MUST BE BORN AGAIN)

The first step to an answered prayer is to have a solid relationship with the good Lord that answers prayer.

<u>John 15:16</u> says, "Ye **have not chosen me, but I have chosen you, and ordained you, that ye should go and bring forth fruit, and** *that* **your fruit should remain:** that **whatsoever ye shall ask of the Father in my name, he may give it you**."

Prayers are routed to God and answered in the name of Jesus.

Therefore, you have a need first and foremost to accept Jesus into your life.

And it is as simple as saying after me;

"Lord Jesus, I receive you today into my life as my Lord and Saviour.

I acknowledge that you died for my sake and rose from death on the third day.

I ask that you forgive me all my sins and wash me clean from all unrighteousness.

From this moment, I have made up my mind to serve you with all my heart without reservation and without holding back.

Thank you for saving me. Amen."

NOTE: You are advised to locate an unadulterated Bible believing

Church to attend regularly in case you have none yet.

CONGRATULATION

PRAYERS FOR EACH DAY- APRIL

APRIL-APRIL-APRIL

DAY ONE (1)
PRAYING SCRIPTURE

1 CHRONICLES 21:1

"And Satan stood up against Israel, and provoked David to number Israel.

And God was displeased with this thing; therefore he smote Israel."

PRAY NOW

I DECREE & DECLARE

Dear Heavenly Father,

I slept and I woke up because YOU kept to your covenant of protection over me, therefore I am here to say thank YOU.

FATHER, by YOUR mercy, I decree and declare boldly that the devil and its agent shall not be able to move me to offend YOU by my actions, deeds and word of my mouth, in JESUS name.

FATHER LORD, I pray that the HOLY SPIRIT in me shall constantly overcome every contrary spirit that wants to shortchange and swap my glorious destiny and position, in the mighty name of JESUS.

For Obedience is better than sacrifice, I receive the spirit of Obedience to YOUR instructions and words which shall move me from glory to glory, from honour to honour, from power to power, from strength to strength, from wisdom to wisdom and from riches to riches, in JESUS name.

The agents of the devil waiting for my down fall and disgrace shall fall for my sake and receive double portion of their imaginations against me, in JESUS name.

I declare boldly that my going out and coming in today is blessed and preserved, in JESUS name.

I cover these prayers with the precious blood of the LORD JESUS CHRIST for performance. AMEN.

REMEMBER TO SHARE YOUR TESTIMONY WITH ME BECAUSE SOMETHING GOOD WILL SOON HAPPEN IN YOUR LIFE.

DAY TWO (2)

PRAYING SCRIPTURE

ISAIAH 44:8

"Fear ye not, neither be afraid: have not I told thee from that time, and have declared it? ye are even my witnesses. Is there a God beside me? yea, there is no God; I know not any".

Psalms 27:3

"Though an host should encamp against me, my heart shall not fear: though war should rise against me, in this will I be confident."

PRAY NOW

I DECLARE & DECREE

Dear Heavenly Father,

I thank YOU for YOUR dependability and that for my sake YOU neither sleep nor slumber. I give YOU all the glory for another day.

It is written that YOU have not given me the spirit of fear; but of power, and of love, and of a sound mind. Therefore, I refuse and reject every power and forces injecting or trying to infuse fear into my life; concerning the loss of my life, my properties, my position, my relationship and any issue concerning me to the opposition and the devil.

I reject every intimidation and I shall not loose any ground to my enemies, by the blood of JESUS.

FATHER, by the blood of the LAMB, I erase every thought and

imaginations telling me or suggesting to me that my dreams, my desires, my miracles, my business, my ministry and my calling will not become realities, in JESUS name

I eject every fear of failures, fear of disappointments, fear of sickness, fear of poverty, fear of helplessness and suffering from my life, in the mighty name of JESUS

I decree and declare that, the fear of the unknown and uncertainties shall not coward me into defeat.

I re-establish my faith in my HEAVENLY FATHER as my provider, my succour, my enabler and the supplier of all that I need.

By HIS power, I and my family shall not suffer dryness and insufficiency.

I shall have more than enough to run my family, to run my business, to run my projects and programs this year, in the precious name of JESUS.

I decree and declare that I shall not be a slave to the fear of what to do and where to go.

I shall be supernaturally directed and guided this year, in the mighty name of JESUS.

By faith and open hands, I receive my portion and allocation of my heavenly benefits for my use and enjoyment on the earth today, in JESUS name.

I decree and declare that my going out and coming in today shall be blessed and preserved, in JESUS name.

I cover these prayers with the precious blood of the LORD JESUS CHRIST for performance. AMEN.

DAY THREE (3)

PRAYING SCRIPTURE

GENESIS 29:31

"And when the LORD saw that Leah was hated, he opened her womb: but Rachel was barren."

PRAY NOW

I DECREE & DECLARE

Dear Heavenly Father, Thank YOU for granting me life.

Thank YOU for another beautiful working week.

It is of YOUR mercies am not consumed.

FATHER LORD, according to YOUR word and its authority, I decree today and request by YOUR mercy, let everything the devil, wicked people and demonic agents have closed down or planning to close down in my life and destiny be reopened this week and very soon, in the mighty name of JESUS.

MY FATHER MY FATHER, let every embargo and limitations placed on my promotion, breakthroughs, business, joy in my family, finances and destiny be shattered, in JESUS name.

LORD, by YOUR mercy and to the shame of my adversaries make a way for me where they have used their mortal power and influence ato block me, in JESUS name.

LORD, I open my hands to YOU, let my divine allocation of Your blessings come to me today and for the rest of this week, in JESUS name.

I decree and declare that my going out and coming in today is blessed and preserved, in JESUS name.

I cover these prayers with the precious blood of the LORD JESUS CHRIST for performance. AMEN.

DAY FOUR (4)

PRAYING SCRIPTURE

JOEL 3:10

"Beat your plowshares into swords, and your pruning hooks into spears: let the weak say, I am strong."

PRAY NOW

I DECREE & DECLARE

Dear Heavenly Father,

I Thank YOU this morning for the breath of life in me.

Thank YOU for sustaining me. I choose to dwell in YOUR secret place because YOU are the MOST HIGH.

I shall abide under YOUR shadow because YOU are the AL-MIGHTY. I declare this day that YOU are my LORD, in YOU I take refuge and trust. I declare boldly that YOU will deliver me from the snare, troubles, war, strife, scourge of tongues of my enemies and from the noisome pestilence, in JESUS NAME. I refuse to be afraid of the people or power terrorizing me, in JESUS NAME. I decree that I shall not be afraid of any weapon fashion against me by night or by day for they shall be rendered useless and impotent, in the mighty NAME OF JESUS. I decree and declare that no sickness and disease shall befall me.

I refuse to be infected and affected by any virus or bacteria and any pestilence or epidemic that goes around in darkness or at the noonday, in JESUS NAME. A thousand may fall at my side, and ten thousand at my right hand due to any reason orchestrated by the demonic forces but it shall not come near me, by the BLOOD OF JESUS. By the intervention of the MOST HIGH GOD, with my eyes shall I see the reward of the wicked coming over them like the torrent of rain, in the MIGHTY NAME OF JESUS.

Because the LORD is my fortress, no evil shall befall me, neither shall any plague come near my body and dwelling place, in JESUS NAME.

Today, I decree and declare that am made whole, am strong, I cannot be down, I cannot be sick, swallowing drugs all the time is not my portion.

I soak every part of my body into the PRECIOUS BLOOD OF JESUS CHRIST to receive strength and be well, in JESUS NAME.

FATHER LORD, give YOUR angels charge over me, to keep me in all thy ways today and all time, in the MIGHTY NAME OF JESUS.

I decree and declare that I shall tread upon the roaring lion of human beings trying to devour me and adder in form of the wicked ones, the young lion in form of the evil doers and the dragon in form of principalities and powers shall I trample under my feet by the help of the LORD OF HOSTS, IN JESUS NAME.

Thank YOU, JESUS, because I called upon YOU, and I have the confidence that YOU have answered me.

I cover these prayers with the PRECIOUS BLOOD OF THE LORD JESUS CHRIST for performance. AMEN.

DAY FIVE (5)

Praying Scripture

Genesis 24:12

"And he said, O LORD God of my master Abraham, I pray thee, send me good speed this day, and shew kindness unto my master Abraham."

Genesis 27:3, 20, 28-29.

"Now therefore take, I pray thee, thy weapons, thy quiver and thy bow, and go out to the field, and take me some venison;

And Isaac said unto his son, How is it that thou hast found it so quickly, my son? And he said, Because the LORD thy God brought it to me."

PRAY NOW

I DECREE & DECLARE

Dear Heavenly Father,

Thank YOU for this day, for this is the day that YOU have made for me to rejoice and do YOUR good pleasure.

FATHER LORD, I have come today to ask for supernatural speed in my assignments and divine purpose for the next quarter of the year, in Jesus name.

By the BLOOD OF JESUS, I receive divine insight, hindsight and foresight concerning my endeavours.

Let my projects, my business, work of my hands, my education, my plans, my spiritual life and my destiny gain divine accelerated speed, in the MIGHTY NAME OF JESUS.

I decree and declare that everything I have lost to any authority, any man, group of people, the devil and his agents shall be restored back to me quickly.

I shall pursue swiftly, overtake gallantly and conquer them powerfully, in the MIGHTY NAME OF JESUS.

By the fire of the HOLY GHOST, I shall find quickly: my peace, my joy, my good health, my prosperity, my good and godly relationships, my fruitfulness, my reputation, my dignity and my balance in life, by the precious BLOOD OF THE LORD JESUS.

I shatter and scatter every obstacle and forces trying to slow me down in any way or manner on my divine race and journey this year, in JESUS NAME

Therefore, GOD, give me of the dew of HEAVEN, and the fatness of the earth, and plenty of corn and wine:

Let people serve me, and nations bow down to me: cursed be every one that curses me, and blessed be he that blesses me, in JESUS NAME.

I receive YOUR divine allocation of my daily benefits today for my satisfaction, in JESUS NAME.

I declare that my going out and coming in today shall be blessed and preserved, in JESUS NAME.

I cover these prayers with the precious blood of the LORD Jesus Christ for performance. AMEN

DAY SIX (6)

PRAYING SCRIPTURE

ROMANS 13:11-14

And that, knowing the time, that now *it is* high time to awake out of sleep: for now *is* our salvation nearer than when we believed.

The night is far spent, the day is at hand: let us therefore cast off the works of darkness, and let us put on the armor of light.

Let us walk honestly, as in the day; not in rioting and drunkenness, not in chambering and wantonness, not in strife and envying.

But put ye on the Lord Jesus Christ, and make not provision for the flesh, to *fulfill* the lusts *thereof.*

MICAH 2:13

"The breaker is come up before them: they have broken up, and have passed through the gate, and are gone out by it: and their king shall pass before them, and the LORD on the head of them."

PRAY NOW

I DECREE & DECLARE

Dear Heavenly Father,

I bless YOU with my soul and everything that is within me and I bless your HOLY NAME.

LORD JESUS, YOU are my breaker, help me to be a pilgrim of faith -

Help me to be a pioneer breaking open new territory and a messenger with a clear word.

Awaken any part of me that is dull or has fallen asleep by the BLOOD OF JESUS.

Release YOUR arms of love upon me and my loved ones today, in the NAME OF JESUS.

Break off the yokes of carnality as I put YOU on, in JESUS NAME.

I declare boldly that I am an army of light and receive the grace to stay in the race of life, in the mighty NAME OF JESUS.

Help me keep my priorities right.

I want to be all that YOU want me to be for YOUR GLORY IN CHRIST.

I decree and declare that my going out and coming in today shall be blessed and preserved, in JESUS NAME.

I cover these prayers with the precious BLOOD OF THE LORD JESUS CHRIST for performance. AMEN

DAY SEVEN (7)

PRAYING SCRIPTURE

ISAIAH 27:3, 6

"I the LORD do keep it; I will water it every moment: lest any hurt it, I will keep it night and day.

He shall cause them that come of Jacob to take root: Israel shall blossom and bud, and fill the face of the world with fruit."

PRAY NOW

I DECREE & DECLARE

Dear Heavenly Father,

It is of YOUR mercies am not consumed and YOUR compassion failed not for they are new every morning and great is your faithfulness O LORD.

Therefore, I say thank YOU.

FATHER, I ask according to the multitude of YOUR love that YOU watch over me and all that belong to me and keep us from the prying eyes of the enemies every moment, in JESUS NAME.

FATHER, come and water everything around me and about me that appear drying, dying and withering or going down below expectations.

Let them all be refreshed, resuscitated and revitalized, in the MIGHTY NAME OF JESUS.

I declare and decree that, I and my children, spouse and relatives in the LORD shall tread upon the serpent, scorpion and adder and they shall by no means hurt us because our feet shall be made of brass and iron spiritually, in JESUS NAME.

By YOUR words and provisions, I shall take root downward into the multitude of water and bring forth fruits and profits.

The works of my hands shall produce and rise above the attacks of the enemies and bring forth in abundance in due time, in the MIGHTY NAME OF JESUS.

I decree and declare that my going out and my coming in today shall be blessed and preserved, in JESUS NAME.

I cover these prayers with the precious BLOOD OF THE LORD JESUS CHRIST for performance.

DAY EIGHT (8)

PRAYING SCRIPTURE

DEUTERONOMY 11:31

"For you are about to cross the Jordan to go in to possess the land which the LORD your God is giving you, and you shall possess it and live in it."

PRAY NOW

I DECREE & DECLARE

Dear Heavenly Father, Great is thy faithfulness, morning by morning new mercies I see. All I needed your hands had provided. THANK YOU, LORD.

I decree and declare that in this second quarter of the year, GOD will take me to my land of breakthrough, in JESUS NAME.

All the powers and personalities that say my glory and destiny will not come to fruition and manifestation, GOD in His anger will send them to battle of no return like He did to Pharaoh and his agents, in the MIGHTY NAME OF JESUS. In JESUS MIGHTY NAME, l decree and declare, GOD shall enthrone me over and above my enemies, all those living like kings over my life shall be dethroned! Any authority in the physical and the spiritual that wants to limit me and obstruct me from possessing my possession shall be totally destroyed, in JESUS NAME.

Everyone going from mountain to mountain from prophets to prophets, from Alfas to sheiks, from witch doctors to herbalists for my downfall shall fall flat before me like the wall of

Jericho in JESUS NAME.

All those who desire to frustrate my life and destiny from crossing over to the next level shall be frustrated by the BLOOD OF JESUS.

Those who thought nothing good can come out of Nazareth were disappointed when JESUS was born, so shall my enemies be gravely disappointed at my breakthrough, in JESUS MIGHTY NAME.

From the beginning of this new month and new quarter of this year, the LORD GOD, will turn my tragedies into triumph.

GOD will turn my setback to comebacks, and shall turn my disappointment to destiny appointments, in the NAME OF JESUS.

GOD will frustrate every satanic plan against my Family, against my Career, against my Business, against my Marriage and Spiritual Life, in JESUS NAME.

As from now, I decree and declare that, I shall make progress by the power of the MOST-HIGH, living triumphantly to the glory of the LORD, IN JESUS NAME.

GOD will perfect that which concerns me financially, spiritually and make me a blessing to myself and others, in JESUS MIGHTY NAME.

I decree and declare that my going out and coming in today is blessed and preserved in JESUS NAME. I cover these prayers with the precious BLOOD OF THE LORD JESUS CHRIST for performance. AMEN.

<u>REMEMBER TO SHARE YOUR TESTIMONY WITH ME BECAUSE SOMETHING GOOD WILL SOON HAPPEN IN YOUR LIFE.</u>

DAY NINE (9)

PROPHETIC DECLARATION FROM ME TO YOU

I DECREE & DECLARE

THAT FOR THIS NEW WEEK AND THE REMAINING DAYS OF THIS WEEK: -

NO WEAPON FASHIONED AGAINST YOU WILL PROSPER FROM NOW ON.

YOU WILL NEVER RECEIVE ANY MESSAGE FROM THE MESSENGER OF EVIL.

YOU WILL NOT MAKE THE MISTAKE THAT WILL KILL YOU

YOU WILL NOT CRY OVER YOUR FAMILY AND FRIENDS THIS MONTH AND THE REMAINING PART OF THIS YEAR.

THE DEATH THAT IS MEANT FOR ANOTHER WILL NOT KILL YOU.

YOU WILL NOT PASS THE ROAD WHEN ITS TASTY FOR BLOOD AND YOU WILL NOT BE INVOLVED IN ANY FORM OF ACCIDENTS.

YOUR BLOOD SHALL NOT BE SPILLED BECAUSE IT IS TOO PRECIOUS TO THE LORD.

EVERY DEMONIC GATHERING AGAINST YOU AND YOUR CHILDREN SHALL BE SCATTERED.

EVERY EVIL COUNSEL AGAINST YOU SHALL BE TURNED TO FOOLISHNESS.

ANYBODY WHO WISHES YOU DEAD WILL GO ON YOUR BEHALF.

WHATEVER OR WHOEVER HAS BEEN ASSIGNED TO BRING HUMAN BLOOD WILL NOT LOCATE YOU OR YOUR CHILDREN.

GATHERING OF TEARS AND SORROW WILL NOT TAKE PLACE IN YOUR HOME.

YOU WILL NOT HAVE ANY REASON TO VISIT THE MORTUARY OR CEMETERY, IN JESUS NAME.

WHAT KILLED OTHERS WILL NOT HAVE POWER TO KILL YOU.

SICKNESS WILL NOT HAVE ACCESS TO YOUR BODY ANY MORE.

GOD WILL UPHOLD YOU WITH HIS RIGHT HAND OF POWER.

YOUR HEAD SHALL BE STRONGER THAN THAT OF YOUR ENEMIES.

GOD WILL MAKE A WAY FOR YOU WHERE OTHERS ARE STRANDED.

YOU SHALL PASS THROUGH THE FIRE AND WATERS AND SHALL NOT BE HURT.

GOD WILL FIGHT YOUR BATTLES AND VICTORY IS YOUR PORTION.

YOUR STRUGGLES ARE TERMINATED FROM TODAY.

THE PAINS YOUR ARE PASSING THROUGH IS DECLARE TERMINATED.

YOUR SECRET TEARS WILL TURN TO JOY AND OPEN LAUGHTER.

YOUR POSITION WILL CHANGE UPWARD AND YOUR SHALL NEVER GO DOWN FOR ANY REASON.

GOD WILL SUPPLY ALL YOUR NEEDS AND TERMINATE EVERY FORM OF SUFFERING, SHAME AND INSUFFICIENCY AROUND YOU.

YOU SHALL NO LONGER NURSE SICKNESS AND THE MOUTH OF DEVOURER IS SHUT DOWN IN YOUR LIFE.

TODAY MARKS THE BEGINNING OF THE BEST OF THE REST OF YOUR LIFE, IN JESUS NAME.

YOUR GOING OUT AND COMING IN TODAY IS BLESSED AND PRESERVED, IN JESUS NAME.

I COVER THESE DECLARATIONS WITH THE PRECIOUS BLOOD OF THE LORD JESUS CHRIST FOR PERFORMANCE. AMEN

DAY TEN (10)

PRAYING SCRIPTURE

HEBREWS 4:16

"Let us therefore come boldly unto the throne of grace, that we may obtain mercy, and find grace to help in time of need."

1 CHRONICLES 12:22

"For at that time day by day there came to David to help him, until it was a great host, like the host of God."

PRAY NOW

I DECREE & DECLARE

Dear Heavenly Father,

Thank YOU for the fresh quarter in the year of my DIVINE GREATNESS.

Thank YOU for victory of the first quarter and for another day added to me.

FATHER LORD, I approach YOUR throne of grace boldly this day by the precious BLOOD OF JESUS CHRIST to receive help.

By YOUR MERCY, even the sure mercies of David, help me day by day throughout this month and this new quarter like you help David, in JESUS NAME.

Send me help from YOUR sanctuary today.

Help me and guard me to run this aspect of race with strength, wisdom, power, and blessings, in JESUS NAME.

FATHER, help my family, my finances, my business, and my

destiny like never before to succeed and have breakthrough this month culminating into big testimonies and celebrations in this new quarter, in JESUS NAME.

I decree and declare that my health shall be at the top shape by the sustainable help of JEHOVAH RAPHA, my healer, in the MIGHTY NAME OF JESUS.

As I appear in Zion today send me YOUR deliverance, launch me into a new realm of holiness and I shall possess my possessions, in JESUS NAME.

I declare boldly that, my going out and my coming in today is blessed and preserved, in JESUS NAME.

I cover these prayers with the precious BLOOD OF THE LORD JESUS CHRIST for performance. AMEN

DAY ELEVEN (11)

PRAYING SCRIPTURE

GENESIS 22:7-8

"And Isaac spake unto Abraham his father, and said, My father: and he said, Here am I, my son. And he said, Behold the fire and the wood: but where is the lamb for a burnt offering?

And Abraham said, My son, God will provide himself a lamb for a burnt offering: so they went both of them together."

PRAY NOW

I DECREE & DECLARE

Dear Heavenly Father,

Thank YOU for another working week.

Thank YOU for I slept and woke by YOUR grace.

With thanksgiving and supplication, I have come to make my request to YOU this day.

YOU are GOD of Abraham, Isaac And Jacob, my covenant fathers; by YOUR mercy and my spiritual connection to them, come and attend to all my needs this month, in JESUS NAME.

Supply all my needs according to YOUR riches in glory.

Let all I need to take off and complete my projects, my business, to pay my outstanding bills, to sort out my debts, to pay the necessary fees, to undergo trainings, to be of help to others and to fund the kingdom projects be supplied to me this month, in the MIGHTY NAME OF JESUS.

I decree and declare that, I shall not suffer for resources to operate with this month and before any need will arise the supply will be adequately waiting, in JESUS NAME.

With strong faith in my heart and outstretched hands I receive YOUR divine allocation of my daily benefits today, in JESUS NAME.

I declare boldly that my going out and my coming in today shall be blessed and preserved, in JESUS NAME.

I cover these prayers with the PRECIOUS BLOOD OF THE LORD JESUS CHRIST for performance. AMEN

DAY TWELVE (12)

PRAYING SCRIPTURE

1 SAMUEL 10:9

"And it (prophecy) was so, that when he had turned his back to go from Samuel, God gave him another heart: and all those signs came to pass that day."

PRAY NOW

I DECREE & DECLARE

Dear Heavenly Father of All Creations,

I thank YOU for the gift of another beautiful day that YOU have made for me.

I ask that every prophecy spoken concerning my life in this new month and quarter of this year shall begin to manifest from today, in JESUS NAME.

I declare that, today is my appointed time and every hanging spoken word of prophecies and prayers concerning my life shall manifest today, in the MIGHTY NAME OF JESUS.

When the cloud is filled there must be a release of rain.

Let there be a release of my promotion, my good news, my miracles, my divine favours, contacts for destiny helpers, landmark transactions and testimonies and spiritual breakthroughs, in JESUS NAME.

I commit my ways and activities into YOUR hands today for divine results, success and fruitfulness.

I shall be established and divinely increased this year, in JESUS

NAME.

I command every force of inhibitors causing delay or lack of results and fruitfulness that I desire be crushed by the angelic forces assigned to me by GOD, in JESUS NAME.

I declare boldly that my going out and coming in today shall be blessed and preserved in JESUS NAME.

I cover these prayers with the precious BLOOD OF THE LORD JESUS CHRIST for performance. AMEN

DAY THIRTEEN (13)

PRAYING SCRIPTURE

JOB 34:29

"When he (God) giveth quietness, who then can make trouble? and when he hideth his face, who then can behold him? whether it be done against a nation, or against a man only:"

PRAY NOW

I DECREE & DECLARE

Dear Heavenly Father,

Thank YOU for this great day YOU have brought me into by the greatness of your power and your mercy.

FATHER LORD, I decree and declare today that, everything making strange noises, boasting and stirring up troubles in my life, in my business, in my working place and family be quiet, in the MIGHTY NAME OF JESUS.

JESUS commanded the raging storm to keep quiet and the storm obeyed.

Today, I declare boldly that, every issue drifting and threatening my life and joy be uprooted and rooted out, in JESUS NAME.

FATHER, by your mercy, let everyone troubling my life and existence be troubled to their bone marrows, in JESUS NAME.

I command sickness, lacks, wants, failures, fears, disillusionments, discouragements, let-downs, cynicisms, hopelessness, helplessness, frustrations, and strange noises be quietened in my life, in JESUS MIGHTY NAME.

I decree and declare that my going out and my coming in today shall be peaceful, blessed and preserved, in JESUS NAME.

I cover these prayers with the PRECIOUS BLOOD OF THE LORD JESUS CHRIST for performance. AMEN

DAY FOURTEEN (14)

PRAYING SCRIPTURE

ISAIAH 52:1-2

" Awake, awake; put on thy strength, O Zion; put on thy beautiful garments... for henceforth there shall no more come into thee the uncircumcised and the unclean.

Shake thyself from the dust; arise, and sit down... loose thyself from the bands of thy neck, O captive daughter of Zion."

PRAY NOW

I DECREE and DECLARE

Dear Heavenly Father,

Thank YOU for waking me up.

Thank YOU for watching over me in the night season and for me not to sleep the sleep of death.

I have come before You today, to refuse and rebuke every regulating powers trying to keep me in the dust where I don't belong, in JESUS NAME.

FATHER LORD, deliver me from any form of mockery hanging over my calling, over my finances, over my career, over my business, over my assignment, over my family and my life, in JESUS NAME.

I decree and declare that, every power trying to abort my joy and happiness; forces striving to change my glorious destiny into pain, be destroyed, in the NAME OF JESUS.

I loose myself from all forms of manipulations working against me in JESUS NAME

By **YOUR MERCY O LORD**, I reclaim my lost ground, I reclaim my divine position and destiny; I reclaim my lost glory and blessings, in **JESUS NAME**.

I decree and declare that my going out and coming in today shall be blessed and preserved, in **JESUS NAME**.

I cover these prayers with the **PRECIOUS BLOOD OF THE LORD JESUS CHRIST** for performance. **AMEN.**

DAY FIFTEEN (15)

PRAYING SCRIPTURE

PROVERBS 25:28

"He that hath no rule over his own spirit is like a city that is broken down, and without walls."

PRAY NOW

I DECREE & DECLARE

Dear Heavenly Father,

Thank YOU for this beautiful day that YOU have made and I shall rejoice in it. O you force, influencing and pulling me back from growing spiritually, I decree your destruction today, in JESUS NAME.

By the BLOOD OF JESUS, I disorganize every spiritual altar and spirit set up to influence me to act contrary and negatively in life.

Every power moving me against God's expectation for my life, negative habits prevalent in my life and every spirit of error, I declare your destructions by the BLOOD OF THE LAMB today.

Every virtue broken down by the devil around me, I decree your reconstruction and restoration, in the NAME OF JESUS.

HOLY SPIRIT, visit me and pour upon me the power of self-control over anger, over excessive talking, over malice, over lust of eyes and flesh, over striving, over Jealousy, over selfishness, over drunkenness, over immorality and carousing, in the MIGHTY NAME OF JESUS.

I receive by the HOLY SPIRIT; joy, love, peace, patience, self-control, and the spirit of holiness, in Jesus name.

I decree and declare that my going out and coming in today shall be blessed and preserved, in JESUS NAME.

I cover these prayers with the PRECIOUS BLOOD OF THE LORD JESUS CHRIST for performance. AMEN.

DAY SIXTEEN (16)

PRAYING SCRIPTURE

ROMANS 8:26-27

"Likewise the Spirit also helpeth our infirmities: for we know not what we should pray for as we ought: but the Spirit itself maketh intercession for us with groanings which cannot be uttered.

And he that searcheth the hearts knoweth what is the mind of the Spirit, because he maketh intercession for the saints according to the will of God."

PRAY NOW

I DECREE & DECLARE

Dear Heavenly Father,

Thank YOU for another beautiful working week and for the ministry of the HOLY SPIRIT.

FATHER, I ask for the help of the HOLY SPIRIT today, to intercede on my behalf concerning the issues of my life.

LORD by the help of the HOLY SPIRIT, come and battle with everything I know or not known around me working against my life and destiny, in the MIGHTY NAME OF JESUS.

Any power attempting to waste my destiny in any way or form, let them be wasted after the order of Pharaoh and Saul, in JESUS NAME.

By the help of the HOLY SPIRIT, I cancel whatever an expert has pronounced against me (doctor, lawyer, prophet, priest, enchanter, sheik, diviner, witch or wizard and...), in the **MIGHTY NAME OF JESUS.**

From today, and by the help of the HOLY SPIRIT, let the Will of God be done in my life with accelerated speed, in JESUS NAME.

By the help of the HOLY SPIRIT, I receive Your divine allocation of my daily benefits today, in JESUS NAME.

I declare boldly that my going out and coming in today shall be blessed and preserved in JESUS NAME.

I cover these prayers with the PRECIOUS BLOOD OF THE LORD JESUS CHRIST for performance. AMEN

<u>*REMEMBER TO SHARE YOUR TESTIMONY WITH ME BECAUSE SOMETHING GOOD WILL SOON HAPPEN IN YOUR LIFE.*</u>

DAY SEVENTEEN (17)

PRAYER POINTS FOR YOU AND YOUR CHILDREN

SCRIPTURES PSALMS 127:3-5,

PSALMS 91: 1- END (Open and Read please)

PRAY NOW

1. My children will not be servants to their enemies.
2. I will not beg my enemy for my children, in JESUS NAME.
3. My seed will not bring me agony and shame, in JESUS NAME.
4. FATHER, let only good things of this earth locate my children.
5. They shall not partake of evil, in JESUS NAME.
6. No evil, stray bullet, sickness will touch my children, in JESUS NAME.
7. FATHER, let it be difficult for the devil and people to explain my movement and that of my children, in the MIGHTY NAME OF JESUS.
8. FATHER, clothe me, I shall not be stripped naked of my children, in JESUS NAME.
9. FATHER, my children shall not be wasted, in the MIGHTY NAME OF JESUS.
10. My children will not be victims of evil substitution.
11. They will not die another's person's death in JESUS NAME.
12. My children will grow up with me.
13. They will marry and have good homes, in JESUS

NAME.

14. I crush the skull of Every Abimelech, Herod and Pharaoh plotting against me and my children, in JESUS NAME.
15. My feet and that of my children shall not step into trouble, in JESUS NAME
16. I shall not be a victim of anyone's error, in the MIGHTY NAME OF JESUS
17. GOD will fight for me and for my children at all times and at every place, in JESUS NAME.
18. I shall not be defrauded or pay any ransom to the kidnappers because JESUS has been our ransom once and for all, in JESUS NAME.
19. My blood and that of my children are too precious therefore I and my children will not witness or experience bloodshed, assassination, accident, crying / tears and pains, in JESUS NAME.
20. My children shall not be terrified, molested, harassed in life, in the MIGHTY NAME OF JESUS
21. I curse every devourer over my children's academics and health, in JESUS NAME
22. LORD, Deliver my children from group afflictions and group kidnapping, in JESUS NAME.
23. I receive and declare championship academically and mentally over my children, in JESUS NAME
24. My children shall not stumble, in JESUS NAME.
25. Place one hand on your chest and the other on your stomach and declare thus: I curse every move and imagination of the evil agents planning against me and my children, in JESUS NAME
26. Every child that sucked these my breasts and passed through my womb /loins shall not be slaughtered by devil's cohorts, in JESUS NAME.
27. I cover my children with the BLOOD OF JESUS for maximum protection, in JESUS NAME.
28. They will always escape the traps of the enemies by

the leading of the HOLY GHOST, IN JESUS NAME.
29. I will not weep or bury any of my children, in the MIGHTY NAME OF JESUS.
30. My children are my garment of honour; therefore, they shall not be stripped off by the enemies, in JESUS NAME.
31. BLOOD OF JESUS, avail and prevail over my children, in JESUS CHRIST.

I decree and declare that, my going out and coming in today shall be blessed and preserved, in the mighty name of Jesus.
I cover these prayers with the PRECIOUS BLOOD OF THE LORD JESUS CHRIST for performance. AMEN

<u>*REMEMBER TO SHARE YOUR TESTIMONY WITH ME BECAUSE SOMETHING GOOD WILL SOON HAPPEN IN YOUR LIFE.*</u>

DAY EIGHTEEN (18)

PRAYING SCRIPTURE

ISAIAH 33:6 And wisdom and knowledge shall be the stability of thy times, *and* strength of salvation: the fear of the LORD *is* his treasure.

3 JOHN 2 Beloved, I wish above all things that thou mayest prosper and be in health, even as thy soul prospereth.

PSALM 112 (Open and Read Please)

PRAY NOW

I DECREE & DECLARE

Dear Heavenly Father,

I bless YOU, I thank YOU for provisions and protection.

I believe in prosperity of my soul and in my body.

Thank YOU for wisdom and knowledge to stabilise my life.

By the BLOOD OF JESUS, I loose myself from every false personality, every double-minded spirit, in the NAME OF JESUS.

I declare that I will be consistent and stable in my life, in my family, at my work, in my character, in my speech, in my thought, in my finances, concerning my health, in my emotion and ministry, in the NAME OF JESUS.

FATHER LORD, by YOUR MERCY, I receive the grace and the power to be a godly, blessed and prosperous person, in JESUS NAME.

I decree and receive wealth and riches, healing and health, deliverance and restoration into my life, in JESUS NAME.

Concerning the giant dreams and plans am executing and that which I desire to undertake, make a great way for me and supply me more than enough of the resources required, in the MIGHTY NAME OF JESUS.

I declare boldly that my going out and coming in today shall be blessed and preserved, in JESUS NAME.

I cover these prayers with the PRECIOUS BLOOD OF THE LORD JESUS CHRIST for performance. AMEN

DAY NINETEEN (19)

PRAYING SCRIPTURE

PSALMS 4:1-8

(GO BACK and READ PLEASE)

                                                                           PRAY NOW

I DECREE & DECREE

Dear Heavenly Father,

I thank YOU for another day in the land of the living.

I slept and I woke up because you have sustained me.

Answer me when I call to YOU, O GOD who declares me innocent, by the PRECIOUS BLOOD OF JESUS.

Free me from my troubles. Have mercy on me and hear my prayer, in JESUS NAME.

Protect my reputation and shield me from false accusations and lies of the enemy, in the MIGHTY NAME OF JESUS.

LORD, set me apart for YOUR glory.

I will not sin by letting anger or any of the works of the flesh control me, in JESUS NAME.

I offer sacrifices in the right spirit, and trust the LORD, IN JESUS NAME.

FATHER, show me better times and Let YOUR face smile on me.

YOU have given me greater joy than those who have abundant harvests of grain and new wine.

In peace I will lie down and sleep, for YOU alone, O LORD, will keep me safe.

LORD JESUS, fight the rest of the battles confronting me headlong and give me victories, in the MIGHTY NAME OF JESUS.

By unwavering faith and outstretched hands, I receive daily allocation of my daily benefits from Your throne today, in the MIGHTY NAME OF JESUS.

I decree and declare that my going out and coming in today shall be blessed and preserved, in JESUS NAME.

I cover these prayers with the PRECIOUS BLOOD OF THE LORD JESUS CHRIST for performance. AMEN.

DAY TWENTY (20)

PRAYING SCRIPTURE

MATTHEW 26:59-60

"Now the chief priests and elders, and all the council, sought false witness against Jesus, to put him to death; But found none: yea, though many false witnesses came, yet found they none. At the last came two false witnesses,"

PRAY NOW

I DECREE & DECLARE

Dear Heavenly Father,

I Thank YOU for another beautiful day that YOU have made for me to rejoice in the HOLY GHOST.

Thank YOU, FATHER, because by prophecy and YOUR confirmed words, this is my season of transformation, my season of redemption, my season of miracles, my season of good reports and positive evidences of Your faithfulness in my life and family, by the BLOOD OF JESUS crucified.

Today, I decree and declare that all powers, people and individuals that are also manufacturing or have devised evil and contrary evidences against me and fulfilment of your words and prophecy in my life to catch fire, in the MIGHTY NAME OF JESUS.

FATHER LORD, by the power that silenced Judas and Pharaoh, come and lay to rest every force and their operators betraying and accusing me day and night both physically and spiritually, in JESUS NAME.

I apply and plead the BLOOD OF JESUS to erase from their memories and files, any negative evidence at their disposal about my past mistakes, errors, failures and the errors of my parents which they can use against me, in the MIGHTY NAME OF JESUS.

YOUR words say, "who shall lay anything to the charge of GOD's elect? It is GOD that justifies.

By the authority of YOUR words, I declare that no power can successfully accuse me this year.

Either in my presence or behind me let the BLOOD OF JESUS show up any time my name is called for evil, in JESUS MIGHTY NAME.

The allied forces of the angelic host shall confront every satanic accuser speaking evil evidences against my life, against my family, against my ministry, against my marriage, against my business, against my finances, against my job, against my career, and Destiny, in JESUS NAME.

By faith, I receive my daily allocation of YOUR blessings into my life for me to run this day successfully, in JESUS NAME.

I declare boldly that my going out and my coming in today is blessed and preserved, in JESUS NAME

I cover these prayers with the PRECIOUS BLOOD OF THE LORD JESUS CHRIST for performance. AMEN.

DAY TWENTY–ONE (21)

PRAYING SCRIPTURE

GALATIANS 3:13-14

"Christ hath redeemed us from the curse of the law, being made a curse for us: for it is written, Cursed is every one that hangeth on a tree":

"That the blessing of Abraham might come on the Gentiles through Jesus Christ; that we might receive the promise of the Spirit through faith."

PRAY NOW

I DECREE & DECLARE

Dear Heavenly Father,

Thank YOU for the gift of YOUR SON, JESUS CHRIST (JOHN 3:16 For God so loved the world, that he gave his only begotten Son, that whosoever believeth in him should not perish, but have everlasting life.)

Thank you for the PRECIOUS BLOOD OF JESUS (REVELATIONS 5:12…Worthy is the Lamb that was slain to receive power, and riches, and wisdom, and strength, and honour, and glory, and blessing.) And thank You for the gift of faith to live with.

By the BLOOD OF JESUS CHRIST, I reaffirm my redemption from the power and effect of curse of the law, curse of any man, curse of the devil and his cohorts and curse of seed time and harvest.

I declare and decree that, every form of curse pronounced against me and household is nullified and erased, in JESUS NAME.

By faith, I receive and appropriate the blessings of Abraham into my life today.

Therefore, I decree that, my destiny is blessed, the work of my hand is blessed and daily, I shall be blessed, in JESUS NAME.

By the shed BLOOD OF JESUS, I declare that am blessed with Power, with Honour, with Wisdom, with Riches, with Strength, with Glory and with the blessings of the earth, in JESUS NAME.

I declare that my going out and my coming in today shall be blessed and preserved, in JESUS NAME.

I cover these prayers with the PRECIOUS BLOOD OF THE LORD JESUS CHRIST for performance. AMEN.

DAY TWENTY-TWO (22)

Praying Scripture

Romans 8:11

"But if the Spirit of him that raised up Jesus from the dead dwell in you, he that raised up Christ from the dead shall also quicken your mortal bodies by his Spirit that dwelleth in you."

John 11:25

"Jesus said unto her, I am the resurrection, and the life: he that believeth in me, though he were dead, yet shall he live:"

PRAY NOW

I DECREE & DECLARE

Dear Heavenly Father,

Thank YOU for making me to know the power of HIS resurrection and the fellowship of HIS suffering. Thank YOU for another day and a brand-new week.

FATHER LORD, by the power of resurrection and by YOUR MERCY, I ask today that every issue of my life that the devil and enemies have forcefully buried to come alive and resurrect, in the NAME OF JESUS.

I decree and declare by the BLOOD OF JESUS and the power that brought JESUS out of the grave that my spiritual life, my health, my finances, my destiny, my buried virtue and all touching my wellbeing and welfare shall come alive again, in

JESUS NAME.

Let everything dulling around me and in me be fired up for better deliveries and greater results, in the MIGHTY NAME OF JESUS.

I declare boldly that my going out and my coming in today shall be blessed and preserved, in JESUS NAME.

I cover these prayers with the PRECIOUS BLOOD OF THE LORD JESUS CHRIST for performance. AMEN.

DAY TWENTY-THREE (23)

PRAYING SCRIPTURE

LUKE 24:2-3, 5-6

"And they found the stone rolled away from the sepulchre.

And they entered in, and found not the body of the Lord Jesus.

And as they were afraid, and bowed down their faces to the earth, they said unto them, Why seek ye the living among the dead?

He is not here, but is risen:"

PRAY NOW

I DECREE & DECLARE

Dear Heavenly Father,

I thank YOU for the wonderful gift of YOUR only begotten son and for the power of resurrection.

Because death could not hold HIM down, I decree and declare that from today no power shall be strong enough to hold me down from fulfilling my destiny, in JESUS NAME.

By the BLOOD OF JESUS, Everything that is dead in my life will rise again, in JESUS NAME.

All my mockers shall be silenced.

Every shackle of limitation in my life is broken.

I shall no longer find occasion to cry and shed tears either openly or secretly, in JESUS NAME.

From today am justified in CHRIST JESUS and the power to condemned me is destroyed, in JESUS NAME.

By HIS death and resurrection, I receive Dominion over all powers of darkness, the work of my hands shall be fruitful, in JESUS NAME.

By the BLOOD OF JESUS, all my enemies shall be permanently disgraced and those who rejoice at my downfall will fall for me because I have risen with JESUS.

Anything that belongs to me that is held down, let it be released to me now by the power of resurrection in JESUS NAME.

I declare boldly that my going out and coming in today shall be blessed and preserved, in JESUS NAME.

I cover these prayers with the precious blood of the LORD Jesus Christ for performance. AMEN.

DAY TWENTY–FOUR (24)

PRAYING SCRIPTURE

GENESIS 24:12

"And he said, O LORD God of my master Abraham, I pray thee, send me good speed this day, and shew kindness unto my master Abraham".

Genesis 27:3, 20, 28-29"Now therefore take, I pray thee, thy weapons, thy quiver and thy bow, and go out to the field, and take me some venison;

And Isaac said unto his son, How is it that thou hast found it so quickly, my son? And he said, Because the LORD thy God brought it to me."

PRAY NOW

I DECREE & DECLARE

Dear Heavenly Father,

THANK YOU FOR THIS DAY; FOR THIS IS THE DAY THAT YOU HAVE MADE FOR ME TO REJOICE AND DO YOUR GOOD PLEASURE.

FATHER LORD, I HAVE COME TODAY TO ASK FOR SUPERNATURAL SPEED IN MY ASSIGNMENTS AND DIVINE PURPOSE FOR THE REST OF THIS YEAR, IN JESUS NAME.

BY THE BLOOD OF JESUS, I RECEIVE DIVINE INSIGHT, HINDSIGHT AND FORESIGHT CONCERNING MY ENDEAVOURS.

LET MY PROJECTS, MY BUSINESS, WORK OF MY HANDS, MY EDUCATION, MY PLANS, MY SPIRITUAL LIFE AND MY DESTINY GAIN DIVINE ACCELERATED SPEED, IN THE MIGHTY NAME OF JESUS.

I DECREE AND DECLARE THAT, EVERYTHING I HAVE LOST TO ANY AUTHORITY, ANY MAN, GROUP OF PEOPLE, THE DEVIL AND HIS AGENTS SHALL BE RESTORED SUPERNATURALLY BACK TO ME QUICKLY.

I SHALL PURSUE SWIFTLY, OVERTAKE GALLANTLY AND CONQUER THEM POWERFULLY, IN THE MIGHTY NAME OF JESUS.

BY THE FIRE OF THE HOLY GHOST, I SHALL FIND QUICKLY: MY PEACE, MY JOY, MY GOOD HEALTH, MY PROSPERITY, MY GOOD AND GODLY RELATIONSHIPS, MY FRUITFULNESS, MY REPUTATION, MY DIGNITY AND MY BALANCE IN LIFE, BY THE PRECIOUS BLOOD OF THE LORD JESUS.

I SHATTER AND SCATTER EVERY OBSTACLE AND FORCES TRYING TO SLOW ME DOWN IN ANY WAY OR MANNER ON MY DIVINE RACE AND JOURNEY, IN LIFE JESUS NAME

FATHER LORD, GOD GIVE ME OF THE DEW OF HEAVEN, AND THE FATNESS OF THE EARTH, AND PLENTY OF CORN AND WINE.

LET PEOPLE SERVE ME, AND NATIONS BOW DOWN TO ME, CURSED SHALL BE EVERY ONE THAT CURSES ME, AND BLESSED SHALL BE HE THAT BLESSES ME, IN JESUS NAME.

I RECEIVE YOUR DIVINE ALLOCATION OF MY DAILY BENEFITS TODAY FOR MY SATISFACTION, IN JESUS NAME.

I DECLARE THAT MY GOING OUT AND COMING IN TODAY SHALL BE BLESSED AND PRESERVED IN JESUS NAME.

I COVER THESE PRAYERS WITH THE PRECIOUS BLOOD OF THE LORD JESUS CHRIST FOR PERFORMANCE. AMEN.

DAY TWENTY-FIVE (25)

PRAYING SCRIPTURE

PSALMS 18:2

The LORD *is* my rock, and my fortress, and my deliverer; my God, my strength, in whom I will trust; my buckler, and the horn of my salvation, *and* my high tower. JOHN 12:37 But though he had done so many miracles before them, yet they believed not on him:

PRAY NOW

I DECREE & DECLARE

Dear Heavenly Father,

Thank YOU for YOU are my rock, and my fortress, and my deliverer; my GOD, my strength, in whom I will trust; my buckler, and the horn of my salvation, and my high tower.

Because THE ALMIGHTY GOD is my rock and fortress, therefore any power of darkness struggling with my life shall not overcome me in JESUS NAME.

I decree and declare that the powers assigned to waste my destiny, collide with the rock of ages and scatter in the MIGHTY NAME OF JESUS.

Arrows of untimely death and any arrow designed and assigned to derail my destiny, by the HOLY GHOST fire go back to your senders and designers in the MIGHTY NAME OF JESUS.

JOHN 12:37. "But though he had done so many miracles before them yet they believed not on him"

FATHER LORD, I know and I believe that Miracles still do happen, let my Miracles defy all natural situations by YOUR MERCY.

I pronounce by the authority of YOUR words, that in all areas that my efforts have proven inadequate let the miraculous take over in the NAME OF JESUS.

I trust and have confidence in GOD that what looks impossible to men will happen for me any time from this moment in JESUS NAME.

I have great faith, expectations and hope that it is my turn to share and enjoy enviable wonders of God this year in JESUS NAME.

By the supernatural acts of GOD, there shall no longer be any delay concerning my affairs and expectations. In this particular period of this year I shall celebrate in JESUS NAME.

Like Joseph, my life will soon become a miracle story in JESUS NAME.

By the favour of the LORD, I shall receive Congratulatory messages any moment from now in JESUS NAME.

I declare boldly that my going out and coming in today is blessed and preserved in JESUS NAME.

I cover these prayers with the PRECIOUS BLOOD OF THE LORD JESUS CHRIST for performance. AMEN.

REMEMBER TO SHARE YOUR TESTIMONY WITH ME BECAUSE SOMETHING GOOD WILL SOON HAPPEN IN YOUR LIFE.

DAY TWENTY–SIX (26)

PRAYING SCRIPTURE

PHILIPPIANS 1:4-6

"Always in every prayer of mine for you all making request with joy,

For your fellowship in the gospel from the first day until now;

Being confident of this very thing, that he which hath begun a good work in you will perform it until the day of JESUS CHRIST."

PRAY NOW

I DECREE & DECLARE

Dear Heavenly Father,

Thank YOU for YOU are my rock and my fortress and my deliverer; My GOD, my strength, in YOU I will trust; My shield and the horn of my salvation, my stronghold.

I earnestly decree and declare that, My GOD will advance me to my next level with favour and victory, in JESUS NAME.

I refuse to be weak, broke and poor.

I am a member of body of CHRIST.

I bear the mark of deliverance, success, surplus, good health, and prosperity, in JESUS NAME.

I declare and decree that, before the end of this month I shall testify of GOD's goodness in a big way.

I confess that I am well able to overcome the giants (problems)

in my life.

I believe that the Greater One lives in me, in JESUS NAME.

I decree and declare that my going out and coming in today shall be blessed and preserved, in JESUS NAME.

I cover these prayers with the PRECIOUS BLOOD OF THE LORD JESUS CHRIST for performance. AMEN.

DAY TWENTY–SEVEN (27)

PRAYING SCRIPTURE

PROVERBS 16:12-16; GALATIANS 5:16-25 (Please Read if skipped)

PRAY NOW

I DECREE & DECLARE

Dear Heavenly Father,

Thank YOU for deliverance over my life.

YOU are strong and mighty.

Extend YOUR glorious hand of faithfulness and blessing to me and my family this day and forever, in the MIGHTY NAME OF JESUS.

Let YOUR supernatural favour be my strength as I commit all my plans to YOU, in JESUS NAME.

LORD, I am calling upon YOU; Now arise and have compassion on me and show me Your favour,

Open the floodgates of heaven. Shower me with the blessings and wisdom that I will have no room to contain, in JESUS NAME.

I bind and rebuke the spirit of the world and all the works of flesh from manifesting in my life, by the PRECIOUS BLOOD OF JESUS.

By YOUR grace, I allow the fruit of the Spirit to flow evidently out of my life to others, in JESUS NAME.

I declare that I am the channel of GOD'S blessing.

Through me many shall be blessed and fulfil purpose, in the NAME OF JESUS.

Am the light of the World, I shall not be hidden.

I shall not operate in darkness.

The Gentiles shall be attracted to my brightness and exploits in life, in the MIGHTY NAME OF JESUS.

I decree and declare that my going out and coming in today shall be blessed and preserved, in JESUS NAME

I cover these prayers with the PRECIOUS BLOOD OF THE LORD JESUS CHRIST for performance. AMEN.

DAY TWENTY-EIGHT (28)

PRAYING SCRIPTURE

ISAIAH 40:29-31

"He giveth power to the faint; and to them that have no might he increaseth strength. Even the youths shall faint and be weary, and the young men shall utterly fall:

But they that wait upon the Lord shall renew their strength; they shall mount up with wings as eagles; they shall run, and not be weary; and they shall walk, and not faint."

PRAY NOW

I DECREE AND DECLARE

Dear Heavenly Father,

This is the day YOU have made.

And this hour is YOURS.

Blessed are YOU because YOU come with messages of grace to save me from my sins.

I just have to be grateful and say THANK YOU LORD.

I have known it and I have heard it that the everlasting GOD, THE LORD, the Creator of the ends of the earth faints not, neither is HE weary.

There is no searching of YOUR understanding.

Thank YOU for constantly watching over me and mine. AMEN

FATHER LORD, I need power to remain steady on the journey of this day. Therefore, ask for YOUR empowerment in order not to faint in the face of adversity and challenges that might come my way, IN THE MIGHTY NAME OF JESUS.

I decree and declare that; my words shall proceed from my mouth with authority and power and thereby commanding situations as desired. When I command sickness and unclean spirits, they shall flee out of their hidden place, IN THE MIGHTY NAME OF JESUS.

Today, and any moment I spend waiting upon YOU, I receive power and authority over all devils and his agents that mighty be waiting for me on my journey to the fulfilment of my purpose in life, IN THE MIGHTY NAME OF JESUS.

I receive YOUR divine power and ability into my life to tread on serpents and scorpions, and over all the power of the enemy: and nothing shall by any means hurt me, IN THE MIGHTY NAME OF JESUS.

I decree and declare that at the face of opportunities, divine advantages, at interviews, during presentations, before the authorities, examiners, and when witnessing to the unbelievers, my speech shall surpass that of natural man's wisdom, I shall flow flawless in demonstration of the SPIRIT AND OF POWER OF GOD residing in me, IN THE MIGHTY NAME OF JESUS.

I decree and declare that I shall not be afraid of any man, any group of people, any contrary spirit because my GOD has not given me the spirit of fear; but of power, and of love, and of a sound mind, IN THE MIGHTY NAME OF JESUS.

FATHER LORD, I receive the grace not to abuse the power and privileges YOU are giving me now or in the future like Pharaoh, Nebuchadnezzar, Herod and our modern-day oppressors in our government seats, IN THE MIGHTY NAME OF JESUS.

Because YOU ARE THE OMNISCIENCE, who knows everything, inside and out.

I ask that YOU energize me whenever I am tired and discouraged on my journey.

By YOUR grace, give me fresh strength whenever I feel like dropping out.

For even young people get tired and drop out, and young men in their prime stumble and fall. But because I am waiting upon YOU, I shall constantly get fresh strength from YOU, IN THE MIGHTY NAME OF JESUS.

No matter how tough the race may appear, I shall walk and run and not be weary until I get to the appointed place for my destiny, IN THE MIGHTY NAME OF JESUS.

I decree and declare that my going out and coming in today shall be blessed and preserved, IN THE MIGHTY NAME OF JESUS.

I cover these prayers with the PRECIOUS BLOOD OF THE LORD JESUS CHRIST for performance. AMEN

DAY TWENTY-NINE (29)

PRAYING SCRIPTURE

JEREMIAH 1:9-10

"Then the LORD put forth his hand, and touched my mouth. And the LORD said unto me, Behold, I have put my words in thy mouth.

See, I have this day set thee over the nations and over the kingdoms, to root out, and to pull down, and to destroy, and to throw down, to build, and to plant."

PRAY NOW

I DECREE & DECLARE

Dear Heavenly Father,

Thank YOU for a new dawn.

Thank YOU for YOU neither sleep nor slumber over my life issues.

Thank YOU for making me a battle axe and for YOUR daily fresh words to me.

By the authority of Your word, I root out every negative word spoken or working against my life, my destiny, my well-being and that of my family. I command them to be nullified, by the BLOOD OF JESUS.

Let all the financial wounds of indebtedness to me and from me to others be healed by the balm in Gilead.

Let everyone sitting on my prosperity and financial breakthroughs be unseated, by the fire of the HOLY GHOST.

I declare boldly that every circle of reproaches, failures and disappointment upon my life, my calling and family be terminated, in the mighty name of Jesus.

Today, I declare by YOUR MERCY O LORD that, my heavens shall be opened this week and I shall enjoy blessings I have not enough room to contain, in JESUS NAME.

FATHER LORD, grant me new and divine speed in all my assignments and plans, and let me achieve results in quick succession, in the NAME OF JESUS.

By faith and great expectation, I receive YOUR divine allocation of my daily benefits today with thanksgiving and for my satisfaction, in JESUS NAME.

I decree and declare that my going out and my coming in today shall be blessed, in JESUS NAME.

I cover these prayers with the PRECIOUS BLOOD OF THE LORD JESUS CHRIST for performance. AMEN.

DAY THIRTY (30)

PRAYING SCRIPTURE

MARK 9:25

"When Jesus saw that the people came running together, he rebuked the foul spirit, saying unto him, Thou dumb and deaf spirit, I charge thee, come out of him, and enter no more into him."

PRAY NOW

I DECREE & DECLARE

Dear Heavenly Father,

Thank YOU for the dawn of a new and wonderful day.

Thank YOU for this working week.

According to Job 22:28, I decree and declare that every satanic authority sponsoring evil against my life be destroyed, in the name of Jesus.

Every foul spirit hanging around me and anything that belong to me, I command your operation to cease, in the MIGHTY NAME OF JESUS.

Every force that has been suppressing my life knowingly or unknowingly, I fire you by the power of the HOLY GHOST to give me room and space to carry out the divine plan of GOD concerning my life, in JESUS NAME.

From this week my testimonies shall be unstoppable, in JESUS NAME.

I declare and decree that, my going out and my coming in today shall be blessed and preserved, in JESUS NAME.

I cover these prayers with the PRECIOUS BLOOD OF THE LORD JESUS CHRIST for performance. AMEN.

BORN IN APRIL?

DEDICATED TO ALL THE APRIL BORN

PRAYING SCRIPTURE

PSALMS 90:12

"So teach us to number our days, that we may apply our hearts unto wisdom."

PRAYERS FOR YOU

I DECREE & DECLARE

Dear Heavenly Father,

Thank YOU for the life of this YOUR child born sometimes ago in the month of April.

I Thank GOD for sustainability of your life and for adding to you a new year and a fresh start of life, IN JESUS NAME.

The GOOD LORD will teach you how to number your days and how to apply your heart to wisdom which is the principal thing in the journey of life, IN JESUS NAME.

In this new year of yours, you shall receive into your life wisdom, which is the custodian of long life, riches, honour, strength, power, glory, and blessings, IN JESUS MIGHTY NAME.

According to DEUTERONOMY 11:21, your days shall be multiplied as the days of heaven upon the earth, in JESUS NAME.

I decree and declare that your days and years shall be prolonged; and you shall not die before your heavenly bound and ordained number of years, in the MIGHTY NAME OF JESUS.

Like David in (1 CHRONICLES 29:28), you shall arrive at a good old age, full of days, riches, and honour: and you will reign on earth, in JESUS NAME.

By the AUTHORITY OF THE WORD OF GOD according to (PSALMS 72:7), in your days you shall flourish; and full of the abundance of peace so long as the moon endures, in the MIGHTY NAME OF JESUS.

In this your new year, GOD will satisfy you early with HIS MERCY AND FAVOUR; that you may rejoice and be glad in all your days, in JESUS NAME.

Because the BIBLE says in ECCLESIASTES 5:18 that, "it is good and comely for one to eat and to drink, and to enjoy the good of all his labour that he takes under the sun all the days of his life, which God gave him:

for his portion;

I declare boldly that you shall spend the rest of your days and years in pleasure in the NAME OF JESUS.

By POWER OF THE HOLY SPIRIT, I decree that problems and challenges that will make the elder to serve the younger never happen in your life, In JESUS NAME.

I decree that, the rod of the wicked shall not rest upon you, in JESUS NAME.

By the authority of GOD'S WORD, I decree and declare that in your new year you shall no longer witness: Anxiety, Breaking down, Borrowing & Begging, Disappointment, Diseases, Lack and Want, Failure of any kind, Frustration, Fruitlessness, Fear and Faithlessness, Barrenness, Depression, Indebtedness, Joblessness, Losses, Loneliness, Mockery and Shame, in the MIGHTY NAME OF JESUS.

In this new year of yours, I Pray for your divine visitations, your new season shall bring to you; uncommon blessings, connections to your benefactors/partners, transformation, restoration and elevation.

Global doors of breakthrough unlimited shall open to you this year.

You shall enjoy Divine Direction and Decisions. Your purpose shall be finally established this year.

You will go higher and enjoy promotions this year.

It shall be your year of unstoppable celebrations and victories round about, in the MIGHTY NAME OF JESUS.

By the anointing of the HOLY SPIRIT, you shall become an "ETERNAL EXCELLENCY" in wheresoever men have written you off and have closed the case.

I decree that, from now onward, good things shall come out of your Nazareth, in JESUS NAME.

Henceforth, every Egyptian that you saw last year, you shall see them no more, in JESUS NAME.

By the POWER OF THE HOLY SPIRIT, your generation after you shall be exempted from the consequences of the wrong and errors of your parents.

Henceforth, GOD'S MERCY will clear all their mess as GOD makes His favour to speak for you in JESUS NAME.

By the blood of everlasting covenant, you shall never venture into anything that will make GOD to forsake you.

I decree that, from today onward, you shall only be involved in things that are right, just, holy, pure and of good reports, in JESUS NAME.

PLEASE, SAY AFTER ME WITH FAITH

FATHER, I bless YOU for the expression of YOUR love to me and family all-round the year.

I witnessed this day 365 days ago and YOU have kept and preserved me. I just want to say thank YOU.

By the prophetic authority of the WORD OF GOD, I pronounce that anyone that shall rise against my welfare and wellbeing in my new year shall fall for my sake in JESUS NAME.

FATHER LORD, I pronounce a balanced growth upon myself and family.

I shall grow daily waxing strong in the spirit beyond the comprehension of my enemies.

I shall be filled with supernatural wisdom and enjoy divine health without breaking down for the next 365 days in the MIGHTY NAME OF JESUS.

IN MY NEW YEAR,

I shall not beg to eat.

I shall not be ashamed.

I shall not be cursed.

I shall not cry over loved ones.

I shall not be mocked.

I shall not be a victim of hired killers.

I shall not be a victim of accidents.

I shall not be sorrowful in JESUS NAME.

I shall be great.

I shall be fruitful.

I shall be victorious.

I shall be celebrated.

I shall be successful.

I shall be favoured.

I shall be blessed in abundance.

I shall be prosperous.

I shall have joy unspeakable.

I shall have peace beyond limits.

I shall make it.

I shall testify to the GLORY OF GOD.

I shall be lifted high beyond falling.

I shall excel in all that I do.

I shall be called Wonderful.

Where the road is thirsty of flesh and blood, I and my loved ones will not go there.

This year, the evils that will happen will not know my dwelling place.

The miracles in the year shall locate me and my household.

My heart desires and expectations will not be cut off.

I will not cry this year, in the MIGHTY NAME OF JESUS.

I cover these prayers with the PRECIOUS BLOOD OF THE LORD JESUS CHRIST for performance. AMEN

TODAY'S PROPHECY

Thus Saith The Lord,

"Through the greatness of My Power, you shall be made a spectator of your own battles as I take over the known and unknown battles targeted to humiliate you."

PRAYERS FOR EACH DAY- MAY

MAY-MAY-MAY

DAY ONE (1)

PRAYING SCRIPTURE
PSALMS 27:1 – 14 (Go Back and Read if Skipped please)

PRAY NOW

I DECREE & DECLARE

Dear Heavenly Father,

Thank YOU for your infallible word made available for me daily.

Because YOU are my light and my salvation and the strength of my life, I decree and pronounce every source of my fear to dry up by the fire of the HOLY GHOST, IN JESUS NAME.

By YOUR word, let every power or force after my life stumble and fall, in the MIGHTY NAME OF JESUS.

FATHER LORD, help me to overcome all form of troubles surrounding me and put all things under the control of the HOLY SPIRIT, IN JESUS NAME.

By faith in the overcoming power of GOD, I crush the heads of my enemies round about me and I shall eternally be above them in all ramifications, in JESUS NAME.

In every area I have been rejected, disappointed, humiliated and mocked, FATHER LORD, surprise me with your goodness and testimonies, in JESUS MIGHTY NAME.

O LORD, deliver me not over unto the will of mine enemies, let every false accusations and evil desires against me catch fire, in the NAME OF JESUS.

I boldly declare that today I shall see the goodness of the LORD in the land of the living, in JESUS NAME.

I cover these prayers with the PRECIOUS BLOOD OF THE LORD JESUS CHRIST for performance. AMEN.

DAY TWO (2)

PRAYING SCRIPTURE

JEREMIAH 29:11

"For I know the thoughts that I think toward you, saith the LORD, thoughts of peace, and not of evil, to give you an expected end".

3 JOHN 1:2 "Beloved, I wish above all things that thou mayest prosper and be in health, even as thy soul prospereth."

ISAIAH 14:27

"For the LORD of hosts hath purposed, and who shall disannul it? and his hand is stretched out, and who shall turn it back?"

PRAY NOW

I DECREE & DECLARE

Dear Heavenly Father,

I thank YOU for YOUR banner of love over me.

Thank YOU for keeping me alive by this hour of the day.

Thank YOU for making my forehead stronger than that of my enemies.

FATHER LORD, by the understanding of YOUR words, I made bold to declare that

only YOUR counsel shall stand in my life.

I curse every contrary imagination, against me and my future, in the MIGHTY NAME OF JESUS.

I decree and declare that, the prosperity of my soul is un-negotiable, I shall be fat and flourishing spiritually beyond any contest from the pit of hell.

I renounce and pull off any filthy garment the enemy has forced or trying to force on me, by the BLOOD OF JESUS.

By YOUR MERCY, I remain a candidate to spend eternity with YOU.

I shall not be distracted from the heavenly race and I shall not be a cast away from YOUR kingdom, by the PRECIOUS BLOOD OF JESUS CHRIST.

Whatever the thief (devil) has stolen or destroyed in my body that may result to ill health, I reclaim and recover it from this moment.

I shall have life in abundance and not suffer breakdown in any of the organs of my body, in the MIGHTY NAME OF JESUS.

Financial prosperity is my birth right and YOUR wish for me.

Therefore, I decree with bold declaration that, I shall not suffer scarcity of funds whenever I need it, I shall be great and not small.

I remove my name from the vicious circle of reproaches, poverty, lack and wants.

I declare the remaining part of this year a period of my unprecedented financial breakthroughs, in JESUS NAME.

No evil is part of YOUR agenda for me.

Therefore, my eyes shall see no evil, my family members shall suffer no evil occurrences this year, in the MIGHTY NAME OF JESUS.

With faith and outstretched hands, I receive my divine allocations of YOUR daily benefits for me today, in JESUS NAME.

I decree and declare that my going out and coming in today and this week remaining shall be preserved and blessed, in JESUS NAME.

I cover these prayers with the PRECIOUS BLOOD OF THE LORD JESUS CHRIST for performance. AMEN

REMEMBER TO SHARE YOUR TESTIMONY WITH ME BECAUSE SOMETHING GOOD WILL SOON HAPPEN IN YOUR LIFE

DAY THREE (3)

PRAYING SCRIPTURE

ROMANS 8:28

"And we know that all things work together for good to them that love God, to them who are the called according to his purpose".

1 JOHN 4:20

"If a man say, I love God, and hateth his brother, he is a liar: for he that loveth not his brother whom he hath seen, how can he love God whom he hath not seen?"

PRAY NOW

I DECREE & DECLARE

Dear Heavenly Father,

Thank YOU for YOU are the beginning and end of all things.

Thank YOU for giving me a brand-new beautiful day that is going to be full of YOUR power and majesty.

MY HEAVENLY FATHER, let YOUR love find expression in my heart and practically in my life.

Let YOUR love be shed aboard in my heart and towards humanity.

I receive the grace to do to others the way I would like them do to me and to treat them the way I would like to be treated, in JESUS NAME.

I place demand on the authority of YOUR word, I decree and

declare that all things shall work together for my goodness for the rest of this month and at all times, in JESUS NAME.

FATHER LORD, let all my conscious and unconscious decisions, actions, inactions, words, deeds and movements work for my goodness from today, in the MIGHTY NAME OF JESUS.

Joseph committed error by telling his dreams to his brothers which led to the fulfilment of his glorious destiny and landed him in the palace.

HOLY SPIRIT, let all my errors this year move me and force me into the fulfilment of my divine purpose and destiny, by the BLOOD OF JESUS.

The bitterness of Haman brought Mordecai from the position at the gatehouse to leadership position with influence, even in a foreign country.

FATHER, let all the activities of my enemies towards me this year lead to my miracle and promotion, in JESUS NAME.

By faith, I receive my daily portion of YOUR benefits to enjoy and run my affairs today, in JESUS NAME.

I declare that my going out and coming in today shall be blessed and preserved, in JESUS NAME

I cover these prayers with the PRECIOUS BLOOD OF THE LORD JESUS CHRIST for performance. AMEN.

DAY FOUR (4)

PRAYING SCRIPTURE

ISAIAH 44:8

"Fear ye not, neither be afraid: have not I told thee from that time, and have declared it? ye are even my witnesses. Is there a God beside me? yea, there is no God; I know not any".

PSALMS 27:3 "Though an host should encamp against me, my heart shall not fear: though war should rise against me, in this will I be confident."

PRAY NOW

I DECLARE & DECREE

Dear Heavenly Father,

I thank YOU for YOUR dependability and that for my sake, YOU neither sleep nor slumber.

I give YOU all the glory for another day.

It is written, that YOU have not given me the spirit of fear; but of power, and of love, and of a sound mind.

Therefore, I refuse and reject every power and forces injecting or trying to infuse fear into my life; concerning the loss of my life, my properties, my position, my relationship and any issue concerning me to the opposition and the devil.

I reject every intimidation and I shall not loose any ground to my enemies, by the BLOOD OF JESUS.

FATHER, by the BLOOD OF THE LAMB, I erase every thought and imaginations telling me or suggesting to me that my dreams, desires, miracles, business, ministry and calling will not become realities, in JESUS NAME

I eject every fear of failures, fear of disappointments, fear of sickness, fear of poverty, fear of helplessness and suffering from my life, in the MIGHTY NAME OF JESUS

I decree and declare that, the fear of the unknown and uncertainties shall not coward me into defeat.

I re-establish my faith in my HEAVENLY FATHER as my provider, as my succour, as my enabler and the supplier of all that I need.

By HIS power, I and my family shall not suffer dryness and insufficiency.

I shall have more than enough to run my family, business, projects and programs this year in the PRECIOUS NAME OF JESUS.

I decree and declare that, I shall not be a slave to the fear of what to do and where to go.

I shall be supernaturally directed and guided this year, in the MIGHTY NAME OF JESUS.

By faith and open hands, I receive my portion and allocation of my heavenly benefits for my use and enjoyment on the earth today, in JESUS NAME.

I decree and declare that my going out and coming in today shall be blessed and preserved, in JESUS NAME.

I cover these prayers with the PRECIOUS BLOOD OF THE LORD JESUS CHRIST for performance. AMEN.

DAY FIVE (5)

PRAYING SCRIPTURE

PSALMS 30:5

"For his anger endureth but a moment; in his favour is life: weeping may endure for a night, but joy cometh in the morning."

PRAY NOW

I DECREE & DECLARE

Dear Heavenly Father,

I bless YOU for YOU are Holy and forever YOU are the LORD. I thank YOU for lifting me up this morning and at all times. AMEN.

Right now, by the provision made for me in YOUR words, I enter into the joy and gladness YOU programmed into this day, for this week and remaining part of this year for me, in JESUS NAME.

LORD, in YOUR favour, wipe away my tears right now, stop anything and situation that has been programmed or in the process of being programmed by the adversaries to make me shed tears over any issue now or in the future.

Show me YOUR mercy again, in the MIGHTY NAME OF JESUS.

I decree and declare in the NAME OF JESUS that, every force and personality regulating or trying to regulate my life unjustly and retrogressively to crumble beyond repair and recognition.

HOLY SPIRIT, provoke a divine recommendation that will change my story for good in this season, in the mighty NAME of JESUS.

By the PRECIOUS BLOOD OF THE LAMB, I shield myself against anything that can cause delay, sickness, failure, disappointment, false accusation, disfavour, bad news and lack of joy in my life, in the name of Jesus.

I decree and declare that my going out and coming in today shall be blessed and preserved, in JESUS NAME.

I cover these prayers with the PRECIOUS BLOOD OF THE LORD JESUS CHRIST for performance. AMEN.

DAY SIX (6)

PRAYING SCRIPTURE

MATTHEW 22:15; 18

"Then went the Pharisees, and took counsel how they might entangle him in his talk. But Jesus perceived their wickedness, and said, Why tempt ye me, ye hypocrites?"

PRAY NOW

I DECREE & DECLARE

Dear Heavenly Father,

I thank YOU LORD for keeping me and for the revelation of YOUR words today.

I stand on the WORD OF GOD today and therefore decree and declare that, every satanic trap that has been laid from my foundation; be destroyed by the PRECIOUS BLOOD OF JESUS.

ANGELS OF THE LIVING GOD, begin to search for and destroy any satanic trap set to entangle my life and destiny, in JESUS NAME.

Today, I nullify and cancel any spoken, negative word that is working or assigned to work against my destiny, against family and prosperity, in JESUS NAME.

By the BLOOD OF JESUS, I raise a standard against any power that is contending for my rightful position in, my destiny, my home, my health, my finances, my family, my office, my place of work, my career and...

I renounce and condemn every scourge of tongue and curses

sent against me, against my progress and general welfare, in JESUS NAME.

Haman was searching to destroy Mordecai but ended up destroying himself; Saul was searching to destroy David but himself was destroyed; Pharaoh was searching to destroy Moses but himself was destroyed; Herod was searching to destroy Jesus but himself was destroyed; Father anyone or group of people seeking my hurt and destruction shall destroy themselves by the same weapon fashioned against me.

Every arrow fired at me and my loved ones shall return to the sender, in the mighty NAME of JESUS.

I receive the grace and HOLY GHOST power to operate above principalities and wicked powers of this world, in JESUS NAME.

I receive loads of YOUR benefits, favours, blessings, breakthroughs, opportunities, spiritual growth, good news and joy everlasting today and especially as I appear in Zion, in JESUS NAME.

I decree and declare that my going out and coming in today shall be blessed and preserved, in JESUS NAME.

I cover these prayers with the PRECIOUS BLOOD OF THE LORD JESUS CHRIST for performance. AMEN.

DAY SEVEN (7)

PRAYING SCRIPTURE

ISAIAH 43:18-19

"Remember ye not the former things, neither consider the things of old.

Behold, I will do a new thing; now it shall spring forth; shall ye not know it? I will even make a way in the wilderness, and rivers in the desert."

PRAY NOW

I DECREE & DECLARE

Dear Heavenly Father,

Thank YOU for a new day and a brand-new moment of my life.

Thank YOU for everything in life.

By the authority of YOUR words, I decree and declare that, this day my:

Anxiety is over

Breaking down is over

Borrowing and begging are over

Carelessness is over

Disappointments are over

Diseases are over

Excuses & inaction are over

Lack and want are over

Failure of any kind is over

Frustrations are over

Fruitlessness is over

Fear and faithless is over

Barrenness is over

Captivity is over

Depression is over

Defeat is over

Error of any kind is over

Insecurity is over

Indebtedness is over

Joblessness is over

Losses are over

Loneliness is over

Low productivity is over

Low esteem is over

Mockery and shame is over

Oppression is over

Powerlessness is over

Pain of any kind is over

Restlessness is over

Ridicule is over

Rejection is over

Sinfulness is over

Sicknesses are over

Sorrow and regret is over

Timidity & slowness is over

Unfaithfulness is over

Unemployment is over

Unbelief is over

Victimization is over

Weeping tears are over

Worry and fretting are over

I decree and declare new things and fresh beginning into my life.

I decree and declare that it is my season of:

Answer to prayers

Appreciation

Advancement with speed

Appearance in high places

Announcement to the world

Breakthroughs unlimited

Blessings without measure

Celebrations

Connection to divine points

Closeness to my maker

Dancing for overwhelming joy

Divine direction and decisions

Excitement and happiness

Enthronement

Establishment of purpose

Eternity with Jesus in focus

Favour before God and man

Fruitfulness and harvest

Freedom and liberty

Greatness and lifting up

Giving and blessing others

Good news and celebration

Happiness

Healthiness and Affluence

Helps from many angles

Inspirations and ideas

Joyfulness

Kingship
Kindness
Lifting
Liberties
Multiplication all round

Month to be amazed

Opportunities and exploits

Praise - fullness

Promotions & going higher

Productivity and results

Quick responses to issues

Release of my desires

Restfulness void of troubles

Reunion with my loved ones

Settlement

Supernatural supplies

Testimonies
Thankfulness

Unstoppable celebrations

Victories all round

Winning battles of any kind,

In the mighty name of Jesus, I declare and pray.

I decree and declare that, my going out and coming in today shall be blessed and preserved, in Jesus name.

I cover these declarations with the PRECIOUS BLOOD OF THE LORD JESUS CHRIST for performance. AMEN.

DAY EIGHT (8)

PRAYING SCRIPTURE

EZEKIEL 37:4; 7

"Again he said unto me, Prophesy upon these bones, and say unto them, O ye dry bones, hear the word of the LORD.

So I prophesied as I was commanded: and as I prophesied, there was a noise, and behold a shaking, and the bones came together, bone to his bone "

PRAY NOW

I DECREE & DECLARE

Dear Heavenly Father,

I thank YOU for this day and for the lives of everyone connected to these prayers directly or indirectly.

I declare, decree and prophesy as commanded over you reading these prayers that, in the MIGHTY NAME OF JESUS for this new day: -

Every calculation of the wicked ones around and against you shall fail, in JESUS NAME.

I prophesy that every plan of GOD failing in your life shall be revived this month, in JESUS NAME.

There shall be restoration of whatever the enemy has stolen, killed or destroyed in your life and family this month, in the NAME OF JESUS.

Anything that represents the dry bones around you shall live well again to the surprise of your adversaries, in JESUS NAME.

No weapon fashioned against you will Prosper from now on, in JESUS NAME.

You will never receive any message from the messenger of evil, in JESUS NAME.

YOU will not make the mistake that will kill YOU, in JESUS NAME.

YOU will not cry over your family and friends this month and for the remaining part of this year, in JESUS NAME.

The death that is meant for another will not kill you, in JESUS NAME.

YOU will not pass the road when its tasty for blood and you will not be involved in any form of accidents, in JESUS NAME.

YOUR blood shall not be spilled because it is too precious to the LORD, in JESUS NAME.

Every demonic gathering against you and your children shall be scattered, in JESUS NAME.

Every evil counsel against you shall be turned to foolishness, in JESUS NAME.

Anybody who wishes YOU dead will go on your behalf, in JESUS NAME.

Whatever or whoever has been assigned to bring human blood will not locate you or your children, in JESUS NAME.

The weapon that can kill you will never be manufactured, in JESUS NAME.

Gathering of tears and sorrow will not take place in your home, in JESUS NAME.

YOU will not have any reason to visit the mortuary or cemetery this year, in JESUS NAME.

What killed others will not have power to kill you, in JESUS NAME.

Sickness will not have access to your body, soul and spirit any more, in JESUS NAME.

GOD will uphold you with His right hand of power and you will stand strong, in JESUS NAME.

Your head shall be stronger than that of your enemies, in JESUS NAME.

GOD will make a way for you where others are stranded, in JESUS NAME.

You shall pass through the fire and waters and shall not be hurt, in JESUS NAME.

GOD will fight your battles and Victory is your portion, in JESUS NAME.

Your struggles are terminated from today, in JESUS NAME.

The pains you are passing through is declare terminated, in JESUS NAME.

Your secret tears will turn to joy and open laughter, in JESUS NAME.

Your position will change upward and You shall never go down for any reason, in JESUS NAME.

GOD will supply all your needs and terminate every form of suffering, shame and insufficiency around you, in JESUS NAME.

You shall no longer nurse sickness and the mouth of devourer is shut down in your life completely, in JESUS NAME.

Today marks the beginning of the best of the rest of your life, in JESUS NAME.

You shall not miss your portion of today's divine allocations, in JESUS NAME.

You're going out and coming in today shall be blessed and preserved, IN JESUS NAME.

I cover these prayers with the PRECIOUS BLOOD OF THE LORD JESUS CHRIST for performance in your life. AMEN.

DAY NINE (9)

PRAYING SCRIPTURE

PSALMS 78:1-11 (Read Please)

PRAY NOW

I DECREE & DECLARE

Dear Heavenly Father,

I thank YOU for taking me through the night season and bringing me to the land of the living today.

Today, I resist every spirit of discouragement, depression, anxiety and worries concerning my dream, concerning my life, concerning my family, concerning finances, concerning business, concerning my career, concerning my education, concerning my destiny, concerning my children and concerning my ...

I will not turn back in the days of battles because victory is my portion.

I claim victory over every form of open and hidden battles confronting me now, in JESUS NAME.

I cancel every plot of the enemy to extinguish and cut my life, my glory and my destiny.

The present issues am facing now will lead to positive testimonies, in JESUS NAME.

The remaining part of this week shall be moment of good news for me because I will experience and enjoy divine results, divine success, divine wealth, divine breakthroughs, divine opportunities, spiritual encounters, divine favours, divine pleasant surprises, divine helping hands, divine support, divine supplies and divine ..., in JESUS NAME.

I decree and declare that, my going out and coming in today shall be blessed and preserved, in JESUS NAME.

I cover these prayers with the PRECIOUS BLOOD OF THE LORD JESUS CHRIST for performance. AMEN

REMEMBER TO SHARE YOUR TESTIMONY WITH ME BECAUSE SOMETHING GOOD WILL SOON HAPPEN IN YOUR LIFE.

DAY TEN (10)

PRAYING SCRIPTURE

ECCLESIASTES 9:11-12

"I returned, and saw under the sun, that the race is not to the swift, nor the battle to the strong, neither yet bread to the wise, nor yet riches to men of understanding, nor yet favour to men of skill; but time and chance happeneth to them all. For man also knoweth not his time: as the fishes that are taken in an evil net, and as the birds that are caught in the snare; so are the sons of men snared in an evil time, when it falleth suddenly upon them."

PRAY NOW

I DECREE & DECLARE

Heavenly Father,

After all my journey and adventures all over the face of the earth, I return this morning to say thank YOU for YOUR faithfulness and love for me.

Am not the swiftest, not fastest or the smartest yet am on the winning side.

This is the demonstration of YOUR love and Favour.

Many gave up and many died but you kept me.

I just return today to say thank YOU, in JESUS NAME.

The battle is not to the strong.

Where the strongest people like Goliath fell in the battle of life YOU fought my battle like YOU did for David.

YOU made me to become a champion over my enemies where they were

determined to make me a prey and shred me.

I return today to say thank YOU for the undeserved victory YOU orchestrated for me, in JESUS NAME.

Many as wise as lion suffered and died of hunger but YOU supplied me with daily provisions and victuals according to Your riches in glory.

I return today and say thank YOU for YOUR MERCY that prevailed over me and my family, in JESUS NAME.

YOU did not allow me and my family members be caught in an evil net nor permit the sons of men snare me in an evil time like we have in the world today nor allow sudden death fall upon me.

FATHER, I just want to say thank YOU for supernatural protection despite all odds, in JESUS NAME.

I decree and declare by YOUR MERCY that, the flow of YOUR Favour and Grace shall not cease in my life and family.

Thou shall perfect all things concerning me and my family, in the MIGHTY NAME OF JESUS.

I decree and declare that my going out and coming in today shall be blessed and preserved, in JESUS NAME.

I cover these prayers with the PRECIOUS BLOOD OF THE LORD JESUS CHRIST for performance. AMEN.

DAY ELEVEN (11)

PRAYING SCRIPTURE

ISAIAH 52:1-2

"Awake, awake; put on thy strength, O Zion; put on thy beautiful garments... for henceforth there shall no more come into thee the uncircumcised and the unclean.

Shake thyself from the dust; arise, and sit down, ... loose thyself from the bands of thy neck, O captive daughter of Zion."

PRAY NOW

I DECREE & DECLARE

Dear Heavenly Father,

Thank YOU for waking me up.

Thank YOU for watching over me in the night season and for me not to sleep the sleep of death.

I refuse and rebuke every regulating powers trying to keep me in the dust where I don't belong.

Let every curse of retrogression directed against me by any force be nullified, in JESUS NAME.

FATHER LORD, deliver me from any form of mockery hanging over my calling, over my finances, over my career, over my business, over my assignment, over my family and over my life, in JESUS NAME.

I decree and declare that, every power trying to abort my joy and happiness; forces striving to change my glorious destiny into pain, be destroyed, in the NAME OF JESUS.

I loose myself from all forms of manipulations working against me.

I loose myself by the blood of Jesus from every incantation, enchantment, evil proclamations and satanic declarations, in JESUS NAME.

By YOUR MERCY O LORD, I reclaim my lost ground, I reclaim my divine position and destiny; I reclaim my lost glory, my lost honour, my lost power, my lost wisdom, my lost strength, my lost riches and blessings, in JESUS NAME.

By faith, I receive YOUR divine allocation of my daily benefits today with an outstretched hand, in JESUS NAME.

I decree and declare that, my going out and coming in today shall be blessed and preserved, in JESUS NAME.

I cover these prayers with the PRECIOUS BLOOD OF THE LORD JESUS CHRIST for performance. AMEN.

DAY TWELVE (12)

PRAYING SCRIPTURE

JEREMIAH 1:11-12

"Moreover the word of the LORD came unto me, saying, Jeremiah, what seest thou? And I said, I see a rod of an almond tree. Then said the LORD unto me, Thou hast well seen: for I will hasten my word to perform it."

PRAY NOW

I DECREE & DECLARE

Dear Heavenly Father,

I thank YOU for the abundance of YOUR provisions and prophecies in my life.

Thank YOU for YOUR word which is yes and amen.

I prophetically look into the rest of this year and my future today and make the following declarations, by the authority of your words.

I decree that, I shall be stronger, healthier and full of strength and energy.

My health shall not be an issue or a concern.

I shut down the mouth of devourer ahead.

No ill health will follow me anymore, in JESUS NAME.

I decree and declare that; my financial situation shall be greater and better than it has ever been.

I shall suck the milk of the Gentiles and the breast of the Kings.

Men will bring unto me treasures and precious things, in JESUS NAME.

Wherever I have been looked down upon and forsaking, I shall become a sought after and eternal excellency and joy to my generation.

I shall become the voice not to be ignored, in JESUS NAME.

I shall enjoy emotional stability; no more bad temperament, no more loneliness and fluctuation in my behaviour.

I shall be totally guided in my utterances and deeds by the HOLY SPIRIT, IN JESUS NAME.

There shall be peace and serenity in my family and no one will be a negative project or a black sheep for the rest of this year and there shall be no loss in our midst, in the MIGHTY NAME OF JESUS.

MY HEAVENLY FATHER, I decree, declare and prophesy that, my relationship with YOU and my attitude towards YOUR kingdom shall be better and more intimate.

No force or influence shall be able to separate me from YOU, in the MIGHTY NAME OF JESUS CHRIST.

I decree and declare that my going out and coming in today shall be blessed and preserved, in JESUS NAME.

I cover these prayers with the PRECIOUS BLOOD OF THE LORD JESUS CHRIST for performance. AMEN.

DAY THIRTEEN (13)

PRAYING SCRIPTURE

LUKE 22:31-32

"And the Lord said, Simon, Simon, behold, Satan hath desired to have you, that he may sift you as wheat:

But I have prayed for thee, that thy faith fail not: and when thou art converted, strengthen thy brethren."

PRAY NOW

I DECREE & DECLARE

SATAN'S DESIRE OVER MY LIFE WILL FAIL

Dear Heavenly Father,

Thank YOU for this beautiful day.

As I pray, I ask that every evil desire that Satan has conceived regarding my destiny is hereby terminated, in JESUS NAME.

Every demonic determination to mess up my destiny and glorious future shall

be frustrated, in the name of Jesus.

By the blood of Jesus, I decree and declare that, every seed of doubt in me to be uprooted, in the mighty name of Jesus.

I decree and declare that, my faith shall not fail no matter the challenges and oppositions coming my way, in the name of Jesus.

O LORD help me to be able to identify people in my life who YOU have already positioned to act as my mirror like JESUS was a mirror to Peter, in JESUS NAME.

I receive the spirit of sensitivity for me to be able to detect every trap and evil plans of my enemies to be revealed to me and make them of no effect, in JESUS NAME.

I ask that YOU do mighty works in my life and trouble my enemies so that they will know that troubling me equates to asking for YOUR troubles.

Let them know they have engaged YOU in a fight, in JESUS NAME.

I therefore declare that their counsel shall come to nought, in JESUS NAME.

I receive today's blessings and favours into my life, in the MIGHTY NAME OF JESUS.

I decree and declare that my going out and coming in today shall be blessed and preserved, in JESUS NAME.

I decree and declare that, surely, God's goodness and mercy shall follow me, all the days of my life and I shall dwell in the presence of the Lord for ever. Amen. I cover these prayers with the PRECIOUS BLOOD OF THE LORD JESUS CHRIST for performance. AMEN

DAY FOURTEEN (14)

PRAYING SCRIPTURES

2 CORINTHIANS 8:9

For ye know the grace of our Lord Jesus Christ, that though He was rich, yet for your sake He became poor, that ye through His poverty might be rich.

PSALM 112: 3

Wealth and riches shall be in his house: and his righteousness endureth forever.

PRAY NOW

I DECREE AND DECLARE

Dear Heavenly Father,

Thank YOU for the abundant grace you have bestowed on me.

Thank YOU JESUS CHRIST and what He accomplished for me.

I decree I am walking in abundance and grace.

I decree wealth and riches is in my house.

I declare GOD'S abundant favour on me.

I declare that whatsoever I lay my hands to do is blessed.

I am a bundle of prosperity.

I shall eat in plenty and be satisfied.

My going out and coming in is blessed.

My finances is covered in the blood of JESUS CHRIST.

I cover my business with the blood of JESUS CHRIST.

My family is covered in the blood of JESUS CHRIST.

DAY FIFTEEN (15)

PRAYING SCRIPTURE

DEUTERONOMY 8:18

"But thou shalt remember the LORD thy God: for it is he that giveth thee power to get wealth, that he may establish his covenant which he sware unto thy fathers, as it is this day."

ECCLESIASTES 10:19

"A feast is made for laughter, and wine maketh merry: but money answereth all things."

PRAY NOW

I DECREE & DECLARE

Dear Heavenly Father,

Thank YOU for this day given to me on the plater of gold by YOUR MERCY.

By the authority of YOUR Word, I pray for my financial breakthrough and abundance, in the NAME OF JESUS.

By the power of the HOLY SPIRIT, release upon me the blessing and power to get wealth this day, in the MIGHTY NAME OF JESUS.

I decree and declare that, YOUR divine power for financial dominion shall rest upon me and my family and bring us to the state of financial rest, in JESUS NAME.

FATHER LORD, deliver me from the manipulations of being financially wasteful, reckless and lack of accountability, in JESUS NAME.

GOD of all sufficiency, come into my life and re-write my financial history; make me a financial pillar in YOUR kingdom with the promise to be faithful in paying my Tithe and giving to kingdom projects according to YOUR blessings upon my life, in the MIGHTY NAME OF JESUS.

I decree and declare that, all blocked financial sources and flows into my life be reopened massively, in the NAME OF JESUS.

By faith, I receive YOUR divine allocation of my daily benefits today with thanksgiving, in JESUS NAME.

I declare and decree that, my going out and my coming in today shall be blessed and preserved, in JESUS NAME.

I cover these prayers with the PRECIOUS BLOOD OF THE LORD JESUS CHRIST for performance. AMEN.

DAY SIXTEEN (16)

PRAYING SCRIPTURE

ROMANS 5:8

"But God commendeth his love toward us, in that, while we were yet sinners, Christ died for us."

2 CORINTHIANS 8:9

"For ye know the grace of our Lord Jesus Christ, that, though he was rich, yet for your sakes he became poor, that ye through his poverty might be rich."

PRAY NOW

I DECREE & DECLARE

Dear Heavenly Father,

I woke up this morning with the attitude of gratitude and thanksgiving looking back at all YOU have done for me.

FATHER, I thank YOU for not holding back your only begotten SON for my sake.

YOUR SON, JESUS CHRIST is the reason for the celebration of my life, for completely taken upon HIMSELF my troubles and woes. Am grateful LORD.

HE was buffeted and punished for my sins and iniquity, JESUS, I have come to say thank you LORD.

The wages of sin is death but Jesus died for my sin so that I might live.

Therefore, I decree and declare that, the power and pang of sin has no effect over me again, by the BLOOD OF JESUS CHRIST.

I decree and declare that, sickness of any kind or form has no portion in my life again, by the BLOOD OF JESUS.

I decree and declare that, my bones and any part of my body shall not be broken by the devil, because JESUS CHRIST already took my place for that, in JESUS NAME.

I decree and declare that, lack and want are not my portion because JESUS already took my poverty away, in JESUS NAME.

By the BLOOD OF JESUS, I terminate hardship and all the works of the devil around me because Satan has no legal right over my life, in JESUS NAME.

I declare to the hearing and confusion of my enemies that am wet and soaked by the BLOOD OF JESUS today and my enemies are helpless concerning me and all that belong to me, in JESUS NAME.

By the token of blood, the destructive angel could not kill anyone in the camp of Israel; I decree and declare by the unspotted BLOOD OF JESUS, that I shall not die but live to declare the GLORY OF GOD in my life, in JESUS NAME.

I decree and declare that, my going out and coming in today is blessed and preserved, in JESUS NAME

I cover these prayers with the PRECIOUS BLOOD OF THE LORD JESUS CHRIST for performance. AMEN

DAY SEVENTEEN (17)

PRAYING SCRIPTURE

1 PETER 2: 2 - 9 (Read Please)

Verse 2:

"But ye are a chosen generation, a royal priesthood, an holy nation, a peculiar people; that ye should shew forth the praises of him who hath called you out of darkness into his marvellous light:"

PRAY NOW

I DECREE & DECLARE

Dear Heavenly Father,

I thank YOU for the brand-new day and for rebranding me for YOUR use.

Thank YOU for YOUR word today.

Now that am more conscious of who I am in CHRIST, I refuse rejections, I refuse discouragement and whatever the enemy has packages for my shame, dishonour and disappointments, in the NAME OF JESUS.

Despite Joseph's rejection by his blood brothers, he still made it to the palace and became a ruler in an unexpected place.

I decree and declare by the BLOOD OF JESUS, that people's opinion of me shall not hold me down nor discourage me again.

Despite the way they see me or what they think of me, I shall breakthrough and break forth, in JESUS NAME.

I curse every attempt of people to make me smaller and operate below my potential and capacity.

From today, HEAVEN shall turn every "NO" they say to me to my "NEXT OPPORTUNITY (NO)" to be showcased to my world, in the MIGHTY NAME OF JESUS.

This year, by the grace of GOD, my story shall be used to encourage others.

By my testimonies, like Abraham, Isaac, Jacob, Joseph, David..., I shall become a reference and prayer points for others this year, in JESUS NAME.

HOLY GHOST, turn my rejection to my selection, my disappointment to my appointment, my cry to my laughter and my pain to gain for my life, for my family and for my calling this year, for am the chosen of the LORD, in the MIGHTY NAME OF JESUS.

By faith in GOD, I receive my daily allocation of my benefits in Christ today for my satisfaction, in JESUS NAME.

I declare boldly that, my going out and my coming in today shall be blessed and preserved, in JESUS NAME

I cover these prayers with the PRECIOUS BLOOD OF THE LORD JESUS CHRIST for performance. AMEN.

DAY EIGHTEEN (18)

PRAYING SCRIPTURE

PHILIPPIANS 1:4-6

"Always in every prayer of mine for you all making request with joy,

For your fellowship in the gospel from the first day until now;

Being confident of this very thing, that he which hath begun a good work in you will perform it until the day of Jesus Christ"

PRAY NOW

I DECREE & DECLARE

Dear Heavenly Father,

I thank YOU for another day which you have made specifically and specially for me.

I choose to rejoice and be glad in it.

I decree and declare that, this is my Season of perfected testimonies, in JESUS NAME

I declare that, for every evil calculation and agenda from the pit of hell targeted at me and family, GOD shall raise a Standard against them, and they shall go back to their senders, in JESUS NAME.

I decree and declare that, in my life, in my home and work there shall be speedy manifestation of GOD'S Counsels, in JESUS NAME.

I receive into my life perfect physical, perfect spiritual and perfect material prosperity and sound health, in JESUS NAME.

I decree and declare that, I shall finish all my projects without suffering any delay any longer, in JESUS NAME.

Today, I shall have testimonies on those long-awaited perfections in my destiny, in JESUS NAME.

With outstretched hands, I receive YOUR divine allocation of my daily benefits today with faith, in JESUS NAME

I declare that, my going out and coming in today shall be blessed and preserved, in JESUS NAME.

I cover these prayers with the PRECIOUS BLOOD OF THE LORD JESUS CHRIST for performance. AMEN.

REMEMBER TO SHARE YOUR TESTIMONY WITH ME BECAUSE SOMETHING GOOD WILL SOON HAPPEN IN YOUR LIFE.

DAY NINETEEN (19)

PRAYING SCRIPTURE

PSALMS 4:1-8 (Read Please)

                                                  PRAY NOW

I DECREE & DECREE

Dear Heavenly Father,

I thank YOU for another day in the land of the living.

I slept and I woke up because YOU have sustained me.

Answer me when I call to YOU, O GOD who declares me innocent by the PRECIOUS BLOOD OF JESUS.

Free me from my troubles.

Have mercy on me and hear my prayer in JESUS NAME.

Protect my reputation and shield me from false accusations and lies of the enemy, in the MIGHTY NAME OF JESUS.

LORD, set me apart for YOUR GLORY.

I will not sin by letting anger or any of the works of the flesh control me, in JESUS NAME.

I offer sacrifices in the right spirit, and trust the LORD, IN JESUS NAME.

FATHER, show me better times and Let your face smile on me.

YOU have given me greater joy than those who have abundant harvests of grain and new wine.

In peace I will lie down and sleep, for YOU alone, O LORD, will keep me safe.

LORD JESUS, fight the rest of the battles confronting me headlong and give me victories, in the MIGHTY NAME OF JESUS.

By unwavering faith and outstretched hands, I receive daily allocation of my daily benefits from YOUR throne today, in the MIGHTY NAME OF JESUS.

I decree and declare that my going out and coming in today shall be blessed and preserved, in JESUS NAME.

I cover these prayers with the PRECIOUS BLOOD OF THE LORD JESUS CHRIST for performance. AMEN.

DAY TWENTY (20)

PRAYING SCRIPTURE

2 SAMUEL 15:31

"And one told David, saying, Ahithophel is among the conspirators with Absalom. And David said, o Lord, I pray thee, turn the counsel of Ahithophel into foolishness."

Acts 5: 22-24 (Read Please)

PRAY NOW

I DECREE & DECLARE

Dear Heavenly Father,

Thank YOU for am a living being.

Thank YOU for deliverance YOU wrought while unconscious sleeping.

FATHER LORD, I pray today that YOU make a fool of my enemies like YOU did to Ahithophel, in JESUS NAME

Let all the Ahithophel of my life commit suicide like the one in the life of King David, in the mighty NAME OF JESUS.

FATHER LORD, I declare and decree boldly that, by the authority of YOUR word that every opposition that has been set or that are planning to set against me in order to keep me bound, I dismantle and set them on fire, in JESUS NAME.

I decree that, anyone in my place of my work that has deployed all measures of the office systems, home system, governmental system and environmental system including policies, as barrier to stop my progress or promotion, let them wake up to find out that I have gone ahead and even become their boss, in JESUS NAME.

FATHER, I ask that YOU do a might work in my life that is beyond my explanation and understanding in the MIGHTY NAME OF JESUS.

LORD, disappoint anyone holding a seemingly important position using power to oppress me, by the PRECIOUS BLOOD OF THE LORD JESUS CHRIST.

By faith, I receive Your divine allocation of my daily benefits today for my satisfaction, in JESUS NAME.

I declare and decree that, my going out and my coming in today shall be blessed and preserved, in JESUS NAME.

I cover these prayers with the PRECIOUS BLOOD OF THE LORD JESUS CHRIST for performance. AMEN

DAY TWENTY-ONE (21)

PRAYING SCRIPTURE

1 THESSALONIANS 2:18

"Wherefore we would have come unto you, even I Paul, once and again; but Satan hindered us."

PRAY NOW

I DECREE AND DECLARE

Dear Heavenly Father,

Thank YOU for fresh breath, for new strength, for new victory over death, for a new day and a new week.

Thank YOU for YOUR steadfast love that never cease. They are new every money and great is thy faithfulness O LORD.

FATHER LORD, I declare and decree on this day you have blessed me with, that every satanic hindrance to my desires and movements be shattered, in the MIGHTY NAME OF JESUS.

I command that every gate leading to the next level of my destiny, my dreams, my marital bliss, my projects, my celebrations, my financial breakthroughs, academic prowess, my exploits, my good health, positive spiritual encounters, and my... be lifted by their own accord or violently broken by the heavenly forces for my majestic passage, in the MIGHTY NAME OF JESUS.

I decree and declare that, every hindrance orchestrated by the enemies and their cohorts against my progress boomerang against the organizers.

They shall be caught in their own webs and snares and fall into the pit dug for me, in JESUS MIGHTY NAME.

By YOUR MERCY and power, O LORD, let every delay I have suffered as a result of hindrances be translated to divine speed and greater achievements for me this year, in the MIGHTY NAME OF JESUS.

This hour and today, by the BLOOD OF JESUS, shall mark the beginning of the destruction of every satanic installation against my life and glorious destiny, in JESUS NAME.

I command the demolition and scattering of forces like that of Pharaoh, Haman, Judas, Ahithophel, Saul, Household enemies, Manipulators and Wall of Jericho against me; let them catch fire, in the MIGHTY NAME OF JESUS.

I declare and decree boldly that, my going out, especially to the place of my work and my coming in today is blessed and preserved, in JESUS NAME.

I cover these prayers with the PRECIOUS BLOOD OF THE LORD JESUS CHRIST for performance. AMEN.

DAY TWENTY-TWO (22)

PRAYING SCRIPTURE

PROVERBS 16:12-16 (Read Please)

GALATIANS 5:16-25 (Read Please)

PRAY NOW

I DECREE & DECLARE

Dear Heavenly Father,

Thank YOU for deliverance over my life.

YOU are strong and mighty.

Extend YOUR glorious hand of faithfulness and blessing to me and my family this week, in the MIGHTY NAME OF JESUS.

Let Your supernatural favour be my strength as I commit all my plans to YOU, in JESUS NAME.

LORD, I am calling upon YOU; Now arise and have compassion on me and show me YOUR favour,

Open the floodgates of HEAVEN and shower me with the blessings and wisdom that I will have no room to contain, in JESUS MIGHTY NAME.

I bind and rebuke the spirit of the world and all the works of flesh from manifesting in my life, by the PRECIOUS BLOOD OF JESUS.

By Your grace, I allow the fruit of the Spirit to flow evidently out of my life to others, in JESUS NAME.

I declare and decree that, I am the channel of GOD'S blessing.

Through me many shall be blessed and fulfil purpose, in the NAME OF JESUS.

Am the light of the World, I shall not be hidden.

I shall not operate in darkness.

The Gentiles shall be attracted to my brightness and exploits in life, in the MIGHTY NAME OF JESUS.

I decree and declare that, my going out and coming in today is blessed and preserved, in JESUS NAME.

I cover these prayers with the PRECIOUS BLOOD OF THE LORD JESUS CHRIST for performance. AMEN.

DAY TWENTY-THREE (23)

PRAYING SCRIPTURE

JOEL 3:10

"Beat your plowshares into swords, and your pruninghooks into spears: let the weak say, I am strong."

PRAY NOW

I DECREE & DECLARE

Dear Heavenly Father,

I thank YOU this morning for YOU ARE MY LORD, the breath of life in me.

Thank YOU for sustaining me.

I choose to dwell in YOUR secret place because YOU are the MOST - HIGH.

I shall abide under YOUR shadow because YOU ARE THE AL-MIGHTY.

I declare this day that in YOU I take refuge and trust.

I declare boldly that, You will deliver me from the snare, troubles, war, strife, scourge of tongues of my enemies and from the noisome pestilence, in JESUS NAME.

I refuse to be afraid of the people or power terrorizing me, in JESUS NAME.

I decree that I shall not be afraid of any weapon fashion

against me by night or by day for they shall be rendered useless and impotent, in the MIGHTY NAME OF JESUS.

I decree and declare that, no sickness and disease shall befall me.

I refuse to be infected and affected by any virus or bacteria and any pestilence or epidemic that go around in darkness or at the noonday, in JESUS NAME.

A thousand may fall at my side, and ten thousand at my right hand due to any reason orchestrated by the demonic forces but it shall not come near me, by the BLOOD OF JESUS.

By the intervention of the MOST-HIGH GOD, with my eyes shall I see the reward of the wicked coming over them like the torrent of rain, in the MIGHTY NAME OF JESUS.

Because the LORD is my fortress, no evil shall befall me, neither shall any plague come near my body and dwelling place, in JESUS NAME.

Today, I decree and declare that, am made whole, am strong, I cannot be down, I cannot be sick, swallowing drugs all the time is not my portion.

I soak every part of my body into the PRECIOUS BLOOD OF JESUS CHRIST toreceive strength and be well, in JESUS NAME.

FATHER LORD, give YOUR angels charge over me to keep me in all my ways today and all time, in the MIGHTY NAME OF JESUS.

I decree and declare that, I shall tread upon the roaring lion of human beings trying to devour me and adder in form of the wicked ones, the young lion in form of the evil doers and the dragon in form of principalities and powers under my feet by the help of the LORD of hosts, in Jesus MIGHTY NAME.

Thank YOU, JESUS, because I called upon YOU and I have the confidence that YOU have answered me.

I cover these prayers with the PRECIOUS BLOOD OF THE LORD

JESUS CHRIST for performance. AMEN.

DAY TWENTY-FOUR (24)

PRAYING SCRIPTURE

PSALMS 78:1-11 (Read Please)

PRAY NOW

I DECREE & DECLARE

Dear Heavenly Father,

I thank YOU for taking me through the night season and bringing me to the land of the living today.

Today, I resist every spirit of discouragement, downcast, depression, anxiety and worry concerning my dream, concerning my life, concerning my family, concerning my finances, concerning my business, concerning my career, concerning my education, concerning my destiny, concerning my children, concerning my health, concerning my spiritual life, concerning my properties and concerning my ...

I will not turn back in the day of battle because the LORD OF HOSTS is on my side and victory is my portion. I claim victory over every form of battle confronting me now in JESUS NAME.

I decree and cancel every plot of the enemy to extinguish and cut my life, glory and destiny. The present issues am facing now will lead to positive results and testimonies in JESUS NAME.

I decree and declare that the remaining part of this week shall be moment of good news for me because I will experience and enjoy divine results, success, wealth, breakthroughs, opportunities, positive spiritual encounters, favours, pleasant surprises, helping hands, support, supernatural supplies and .... in JESUS NAME.

I declare boldly that my going out and coming in today is divinely blessed and supernaturally preserved in JESUS NAME.

I cover these prayers with the PRECIOUS BLOOD OF THE LORD JESUS CHRIST for performance. AMEN.

DAY TWENTY-FIVE (25)

PRAYING SCRIPTURE

GENESIS 28:10-22 (Read Please)

KEY VERSE: 15 NKJV

"Behold, I am with you and will keep you wherever you go, and will bring you back to this land; for I will not leave you until I have done what I have spoken to you."

PRAY NOW

I DECREE & DECLARE

Dear Heavenly Father,

I thank YOU.

I worship and commit my heart, soul and body to YOU.

Let YOUR fresh power of the HOLY SPIRIT begin to operate in my life like a strong wind and break me free from the bondage of sin and death, by the BLOOD OF JESUS CHRIST.

I decree and pray for a shift in the atmosphere this year for the release and the flow of blessing, glory, power, wisdom, riches and miracles into my life – into my family, into my work and ministry, in the NAME OF JESUS.

By faith, I decree and declare that I will see the fulfilment of covenant promises and prophecies of GOD'S word in my life - supernatural preservation, protection, provision and promotion, in JESUS NAME.

Make me a man/woman after your heart, a house of prayer - the gateway of HEAVEN and the citadel of YOUR GLORY, IN JESUS MIGHTY NAME.

I decree and declare that, I am untouchable by lack, sickness and all oppression of the enemy, in the MIGHTY NAME OF JESUS.

I receive an Impartation of the spirit of holiness and wisdom today, in the MIGHTY NAME OF JESUS.

I boldly declare in the LORD that my going out and coming in today shall be blessed and preserved, in JESUS NAME.

I cover these prayers with the PRECIOUS BLOOD OF THE LORD JESUS CHRIST for performance. AMEN

REMEMBER TO SHARE YOUR TESTIMONY WITH ME BECAUSE SOMETHING GOOD WILL SOON HAPPEN IN YOUR LIFE.

DAY TWENTY-SIX (26)

PRAYING SCRIPTURE

PSALMS 23:1-6

"The LORD is my shepherd; I shall not want.

He maketh me to lie down in green pastures: he leadeth me beside the still waters.

He restoreth my soul: he leadeth me in the paths of righteousness for his name's sake.Yea, though I walk through the valley of the shadow of death, I will fear no evil: for thou art with me; thy rod and thy staff they comfort me.Thou preparest a table before me in the presence of mine enemies: thou anointest my head with oil; my cup runneth over.Surely goodness and mercy shall follow me all the days of my life: and I will dwell in the house of the LORD for ever."

PRAY NOW

I DECREE & DECLARE

Dear Heavenly Father,

Thank YOU for being there for me. Thank YOU for another day and the just concluded weekend.

FATHER, I receive divine direction concerning all the issues of my life and for spending the rest of this month, in JESUS NAME.

I curse every spirit of lack and want to whither from the root out of my life and family and let there be restoration of anything we have lost, in the MIGHTY NAME OF JESUS.

By Your divine guidance lead me the way I should go; I shall not run or walk into trouble with GOD, the authority over me, or anyone else that will attract punishment or penalty, in the NAME OF JESUS.

I rebuke and curse the spirit of fear that has crept into my life today and I receive the grace, mercy, love and joy unspeakable into my life and family, in JESUS NAME.

I decree and declare that, for the rest of this year and my entire life the anointing of the HOLY SPIRIT will make me stronger, healthier, better and richer, in JESUS NAME.

Despite the wicked imaginations of my enemies, GOD shall provide for me and my family in abundance and we shall have enough to give out, in JESUS NAME.

Surely and without debate only your goodness and mercy shall follow me, prosperity, good health, joy, peace, celebrations, blessings, spiritual in depth and victories for the rest of this year, in the MIGHTY NAME OF JESUS.

I decree and declare that, the MERCY OF THE LORD, my going out and coming in today shall be blessed and preserved, in JESUS NAME.

I cover these prayers with the PRECIOUS BLOOD OF THE LORD JESUS CHRIST for performance. AMEN.

DAY TWENTY-SEVEN (27)

PRAYING SCRIPTURE

LUKE 22:31-34

" And the Lord said, Simon, Simon, behold, Satan hath desired to have you, that he may sift you as wheat:

But I have prayed for thee, that thy faith fail not: and when thou art converted, strengthen thy brethren.

And he said unto him, Lord, I am ready to go with thee, both into prison, and to death.

And he said, I tell thee, Peter, the cock shall not crow this day, before that thou shalt thrice deny that thou knowest me."

PRAY NOW

I DECREE & DECLARE

Dear Heavenly Father,

Whenever I see another breaking of the day, I say thank YOU LORD.

Today, I ask for strength to continuously maintain a consistent life of fasting, prayer and the study of YOUR Word so that I don't go back into my old ways, in JESUS NAME.

I declare, I will continue to pursue GOD and grow in faith and never deny YOU no matter the circumstances, in the MIGHTY NAME OF JESUS.

I ask YOU locate people around me who can point to me when am going astray, and I ask for the spirit of humility and a listening ear to listen when I am going astray, in JESUS NAME.

YOU changed name for Peter to fulfil destiny.

FATHER, deliver me from every negative influence associated with my former or family name by the BLOOD OF JESUS.

I soak myself into the PRECIOUS BLOOD OF JESUS and decree that I shall no longer be vulnerable to the tricks and devices of the devil and my enemies, in JESUS NAME.

By faith, I receive YOUR divine allocation of my daily benefits today and I shall not lack nor suffer wants, in JESUS NAME.

I declare that my going out and my coming in today shall be blessed and preserved, in JESUS NAME.

I cover these prayers with the PRECIOUS BLOOD OF THE LORD JESUS CHRIST for performance.

DAY TWENTY-EIGHT (28)

PRAYING SCRIPTURE

1 CHRONICLES 12:21-22

" And they helped David against the band of the rovers: for they were all mighty men of valour, and were captains in the host.

For at that time day by day there came to David to help him, until it was a great host, like the host of God."

PRAY NOW

I DECREE & DECLARE

Dear Heavenly Father,

Thank YOU for this great day and another new week that YOU have made for my joy and gladness.

I praise YOU for the breath of life.

FATHER LORD, today is the day of favour, mercy, grace and helps.

By YOUR mercy and by my faith in YOU, I receive helps in all my endeavours in this new day, in JESUS NAME.

I decree and declare that, all creatures will help me in all ramifications.

When I need financial helps relevant men and women with relevant information and resources shall come up, in JESUS

NAME.

When I need to confront a situation headlong, mighty men of valour will show up to help me, in JESUS NAME.

When I need spiritual intervention, the intercessors starting from my LORD JESUS, THE HOLY SPIRIT, just men made perfect and men assigned by GOD to watch over this nation shall rise up on my behalf and help me, in the MIGHTY NAME OF JESUS.

Moon doesn't have light by itself but shines by correctly positioning itself with the Sun.

FATHER LORD, I decree and declare by the BLOOD OF JESUS that nothing shall shift my positioning with YOU for day by day help, in the MIGHTY NAME OF JESUS.

By faith I receive my daily loads of benefits today, in JESUS NAME.

I decree and declare that my going out and coming in today shall be blessed and preserved, in JESUS NAME.

I cover these prayers with the PRECIOUS BLOOD OF THE LORD JESUS CHRIST for performance. AMEN

DAY TWENTY-NINE (29)

PRAYING SCRIPTURE

PSALMS 30:5

"For his anger endureth but a moment; in his favour is life: weeping may endure for a night, but joy cometh in the morning."

PRAY NOW

I DECREE & DECLARE

Dear Heavenly Father,

I bless YOU for YOU are HOLY and forever YOU are the LORD.

I thank YOU for lifting me up this morning and at all times. AMEN.

Right now, by the provision made for me in YOUR words, I enter into the joy and gladness YOU programmed into this day, and the remaining part of this year for me, in JESUS NAME.

LORD, in Your favour, wipe away my tears right now, stop anything and situation that has been programmed or in the process of being programmed by the adversaries to make me shed tears over any issue now or in the future.

Show me YOUR MERCY again, in the MIGHTY NAME OF JESUS.

I decree and declare in the NAME OF JESUS, that, every force and personality regulating or trying to regulate my life unjustly and retrogressively to crumble beyond repair, in JESUS

NAME.

I decree that every power prolonging the manifestation of my testimony to be shattered.

Every form of delay and setback in my life and family shall receive divine speed, in JESUS NAME.

HOLY SPIRIT, provoke a divine recommendation that will change my story for good, this season, in JESUS NAME.

By the PRECIOUS BLOOD OF THE LAMB, I shield myself against anything that can cause delay, sickness, failure, disappointment, false accusation, disfavour, bad news and lack of joy in my life, in JESUS NAME.

I decree and declare that, my going out and coming in today shall be blessed and preserved, in JESUS NAME.

I cover these prayers with the PRECIOUS BLOOD OF THE LORD JESUS CHRIST for performance. AMEN

DAY THIRTY (30)

PRAYING SCRIPTURE

ISAIAH 30:21

"And thine ears shall hear a word behind thee, saying, This is the way, walk ye in it, when ye turn to the right hand, and when ye turn to the left."

PRAY NOW

I DECREE & DECLARE

Dear Heavenly Father,

I thank YOU because YOU are my Shepherd and I shall not want.

Thank YOU for making me to lie down and bringing me up in peace and one piece this day.

FATHER, it is one thing to desire and determine to get to a particular destination, to achieve a purpose and to arrive at a point; But another thing is to know the direction and how to arrive there.

I receive divine directions concerning all my journeys, concerning all my desires

and assignments for the remaining part of this year.

I shall not suffer confusion nor waste my time, nor waste my divine

opportunities, nor waste my investments, nor waste my resources and energy in wrong directions, in JESUS NAME.

FATHER LORD, lead me in the right paths and paths of righteousness for the remaining part of this year. In everything am doing or I have done wrongly, by YOUR MERCY restore me quickly lest I become a reproach, a failure, a Waster and a wanderer, in JESUS NAME.

I decree and declare that my teachers shall no longer be removed into a corner anymore and both my spiritual and physical ears shall remain sensitive to hear YOUR words, to pick directions and instructions from the Holy Spirit, in Jesus name.

I receive the help of my guiding ANGEL.

I declare and pronounce that, I shall not be confused any longer over any matter touching my life, touching my family, touching my destiny, touching my ministry, touching my finances, touching my business, touching my health, and touching issues where I need to make choices, in the MIGHTY NAME OF JESUS.

I plead the BLOOD OF JESUS and Sanctify the length, breath, height and depth of

my journey for the rest of this week.

I shall not walk into trouble, error or any situation that will permit my enemies to laugh at me, in JESUS NAME.

By faith, I receive my loads of YOUR benefits and every provision I will need to run the remaining race of the week effectively and efficiently today, in JESUS NAME.

I decree and declare that my going out and coming in today shall be blessed and preserved, by the blood and in the NAME OF JESUS.

I cover these prayers with the PRECIOUS BLOOD OF THE LORD JESUS CHRIST for performance. AMEN.

DAY THIRTY-ONE (31)

PRAYING SCRIPTURE

MATTHEW 22:15, 18

"Then went the Pharisees, and took counsel how they might entangle him in his talk.

But Jesus perceived their wickedness, and said, Why tempt ye me, ye hypocrites?"

PRAY NOW

I DECREE & DECLARE

Dear Heavenly Father,

I thank YOU Lord for keeping me and for the revelation of YOUR words today.

I stand on the WORD OF GOD today and therefore, decree and declare every satanic trap that has been set from my foundation; be destroyed, by the PRECIOUS BLOOD OF JESUS.

ANGELS OF THE LIVING GOD, begin to search for and destroy any satanic trap and snare set to entangle my destiny and hold me captive, in JESUS NAME.

Today, I nullify and cancel any spoken negative word, aspersions, divination and incantation that is working against my destiny and family, in JESUS NAME.

BLOOD OF JESUS (3X), set a standard against any power that is contending for my rightful position in my destiny, health, finances, family, office, place of work, career and... in JESUS NAME

I renounce and condemn every scourge of tongues, curse of man, satanic curse and curse of seed time and harvest against me, in JESUS NAME.

I receive the grace, mercy and HOLY GHOST power to operate above principalities and wicked powers that fly both in the day and night in this world and in my areas of influence, in JESUS NAME.

I receive loads of YOUR benefits, favours, blessings, breakthroughs, opportunities, spiritual growth, good news and joy everlasting today, in JESUS NAME.

I decree and declare that, my going out and coming in today shall be blessed and preserved, in JESUS NAME.

I cover these prayers with the PRECIOUS BLOOD OF THE LORD JESUS CHRIST for performance. AMEN.

BORN IN MAY?

DEDICATED TO ALL THE MAY BORN

PRAYING SCRIPTURE

PSALMS 90:12

"So teach us to number our days, that we may apply our hearts unto wisdom."

PRAYERS FOR YOU

I DECREE AND DECLARE

Dear Heavenly Father,

Thank YOU for the life of this YOUR child born sometimes ago in the month of May.

I Thank GOD for sustainability of your life and for adding to you a new year and a fresh start of life, IN JESUS NAME.

The GOOD LORD will teach you how to number your days and how to apply your heart to wisdom which is the principal thing in the journey of life, IN JESUS NAME.

In this new year of yours, you shall receive into your life wisdom, which is the custodian of long life, riches, honour, strength, power, glory, and blessings, IN JESUS MIGHTY NAME.

According to DEUTERONOMY 11:21, your days shall be multiplied as the days of heaven upon the earth, in JESUS NAME.

I decree and declare that your days and years shall be prolonged; and you shall not die before your heavenly bound and ordained number of years, in the MIGHTY NAME OF JESUS.

Like David in (1 CHRONICLES 29:28), you shall arrive at a good old age, full of days, riches, and honour: and you will reign on earth, in JESUS NAME.

By the AUTHORITY OF THE WORD OF GOD according to (PSALMS 72:7), in your days you shall flourish; and full of the abundance of peace so long as the moon endures, in the MIGHTY NAME OF JESUS.

In this your new year, GOD will satisfy you early with HIS MERCY AND FAVOUR; that you may rejoice and be glad in all your days, in JESUS NAME.

Because the BIBLE says in ECCLESIASTES 5:18 that, "it is good and comely for one to eat and to drink, and to enjoy the good of all his labour that he takes under the sun all the days of his life, which God gave him: for his portion;

I declare boldly that you shall spend the rest of your days and years in pleasure in the NAME OF JESUS.

By POWER OF THE HOLY SPIRIT, I decree that problems and challenges that will make the elder to serve the younger never happen in your life, In JESUS NAME.

I decree that, the rod of the wicked shall not rest upon you, in JESUS NAME.

By the authority of GOD'S WORD, I decree and declare that in your new year you shall no longer witness: Anxiety, Breaking down, Borrowing & Begging, Disappointment, Diseases, Lack and Want, Failure of any kind, Frustration, Fruitlessness, Fear and Faithlessness, Barrenness, Depression, Indebtedness, Joblessness, Losses, Loneliness, Mockery and Shame, in the MIGHTY NAME OF JESUS.

In this new year of yours, I Pray for your divine visitations, your new season shall bring to you; uncommon blessings, connections to your benefactors/partners, transformation, restoration and elevation.

Global doors of breakthrough unlimited shall open to you this year.

You shall enjoy Divine Direction and Decisions. Your purpose shall be finally established this year.

You will go higher and enjoy promotions this year.

It shall be your year of unstoppable celebrations and victories round about, in the MIGHTY NAME OF JESUS.

By the anointing of the HOLY SPIRIT, you shall become an "ETERNAL EXCELLENCY" wheresoever men have written you off and have closed the case.

I decree that, from now onward, good things shall come out of your Nazareth, in JESUS NAME.

Henceforth, every Egyptian that you saw last year, you shall see them no more, in JESUS NAME.

By the POWER OF THE HOLY SPIRIT, your generation after you shall be exempted from the consequences of the wrong and errors of your parents.

Henceforth, GOD'S MERCY will clear all their mess as GOD makes His favour to speak for you in JESUS NAME.

By the blood of everlasting covenant, you shall never venture into anything that will make GOD to forsake you.

I decree that, from today onward, you shall only be involved in things that are right, just, holy, pure and of good reports, in JESUS NAME.

PLEASE, SAY AFTER ME WITH FAITH

FATHER, I bless YOU for the expression of YOUR love to me and family all-round the year.

I witnessed this day 365 days ago and YOU have kept and preserved me. I just want to say thank YOU.

By the prophetic authority of the WORD OF GOD, I pronounce that anyone that shall rise against my welfare and wellbeing in my new year shall fall for my sake in JESUS NAME.

FATHER LORD, I pronounce a balanced growth upon myself and family.

I shall grow daily waxing strong in the spirit beyond the comprehension of my enemies.

I shall be filled with supernatural wisdom and enjoy divine health without breaking down for the next 365 days in the MIGHTY NAME OF JESUS.

IN MY NEW YEAR,

I shall not beg to eat.

I shall not be ashamed.

I shall not be cursed.

I shall not cry over loved ones.

I shall not be mocked.

I shall not be a victim of hired killers.

I shall not be a victim of accidents.

I shall not be sorrowful in JESUS NAME.

I shall be great.

I shall be fruitful.

I shall be victorious.

I shall be celebrated.

I shall be successful.

I shall be favoured.

I shall be blessed in abundance.

I shall be prosperous.

I shall have joy unspeakable.

I shall have peace beyond limits.

I shall make it.

I shall testify to the GLORY OF GOD.

I shall be lifted high beyond falling.

I shall excel in all that I do.

I shall be called Wonderful.

Where the road is thirsty of flesh and blood, I and my loved ones will not go there.

This year, the evils that will happen will not know my dwelling place.

The miracles in the year shall locate me and my household.

My heart desires and expectations will not be cut off.

I will not cry this year, in the MIGHTY NAME OF JESUS.

I cover these prayers with the PRECIOUS BLOOD OF THE LORD JESUS CHRIST for performance. AMEN

TODAY'S PROPHECY

Thus Saith The Lord,

"Through the greatness of My Power, you shall be made a spectator of your own battles as I take over the known and unknown battles targeted to humiliate you."

PRAYERS FOR EACH DAY- JUNE

JUNE-JUNE-JUNE

DAY ONE (1)

PRAYING SCRIPTURE

JUDGES 14:5-6, 8-9, 14

"Then went Samson down, ... And, behold, a young lion roared against him. And the spirit of the lord came mightily upon him, and he rent him as he would have rent a kid, and he had nothing in his hand: ...And after a time he returned..., and he turned aside to see the carcase of the lion: and, behold, there was a swarm of bees and honey in the carcase of the lion. And he took thereof in his hands, and went on eating, and came to his father and mother, and he gave them, and they did eat: ... And he said unto them, out of the eater came forth meat, and out of the strong came forth sweetness...

PRAY NOW

I DECREE & DECLARE

Dear Heavenly Father,

I praise YOUR name for another beautiful day and for the enablement of YOUR HOLY SPIRIT in me.

FATHER LORD, by the authority and potency of today's scripture, I decree and declare that, every situation challenging me shall become a walk over and turn to my advantages, in JESUS NAME.

I declare that every scary situation of my life right now will bring the best out of me and turn me to a bold superstar and a celebrity, in JESUS NAME.

FATHER, I pronounce with my first breath today that everything that is seemingly sour, tasteless or bitter in my life shall turn to my delight, to my comfort and sweetness, in JESUS NAME.

I shall pursue, overtake, conquer my enemies and always return with booties and the goodness of the LORD, in JESUS NAME.

I shall have more than enough blessings to honour my parents and anyone standing as my parents, in the MIGHTY NAME OF JESUS.

Let every defeat and scary situation of my life turn to victory; every problem to turn to my promotion; every shame turn to my honour; every challenge turn to my positive change; every failure turn to my success; my trials shall turn to testimonies; my hardship shall turn to breaking forth, and I declare that everything shall work in my favour, in the MIGHTY NAME OF JESUS.

For my shame I shall receive double honour.

My dryness shall turn to fruitfulness.

Obstacles in my life shall turn to my testimonies.

I shall take root downward and bring forth fruits upward, in JESUS NAME.

I decree and declare that, my going out and coming in today shall be blessed and preserved, in JESUS NAME.

I cover these prayers with the PRECIOUS BLOOD OF THE LORD JESUS CHRIST for performance. AMEN.

REMEMBER TO SHARE YOUR TESTIMONY WITH ME BECAUSE SOMETHING GOOD WILL SOON HAPPEN IN YOUR LIFE.

DAY TWO (2)

PRAYING SCRIPTURE

2 SAMUEL 6:9-11

"And David was afraid of the LORD that day, and said, How shall the ark of the LORD come to me?

So David would not remove the ark of the LORD unto him into the city of David: but David carried it aside into the house of Obededom the Gittite.

And the ark of the LORD continued in the house of Obededom the Gittite three months: and the LORD blessed Obededom, and all his household."

PRAY NOW

I DECREE & DECLARE

Dear Heavenly Father,

Thank YOU for your grace and mercy over me and my household.
Thank YOU for your words and divine revelations today.

LORD, by Your favour, terminate my financial struggles.

I file - in after the order of Obededom for sorrow free blessings for the rest of this year in JESUS NAME.

It took only three months to terminate the untold family financial pressure of Obededom; And because what YOU did for one, YOU are capable of doing for others, I therefore decree and declare that, my financial situation shall witness an unprecedented explosion in this week, in the MIGHTY NAME OF JESUS.

FATHER, let pressure, fear of the unknown and ignorance of others turn to my divine opportunities leading them to push the hiding treasures of the earth to me and my family, in the MIGHTY NAME OF JESUS.

Let the negative intentions of the people to harm me turn to my divine greatness this year and what is killing others (like Uzzah, who touched the Ark and died) will not know my dwelling place, in the MIGHTY NAME OF JESUS.

I receive YOUR divine allocation of my daily benefits today with great faith and expectation, in JESUS NAME.

I declare by the BLOOD OF JESUS that my going out and my coming in today is blessed, secured, protected and preserved in JESUS NAME.

I cover these prayers with the PRECIOUS BLOOD OF THE LORD JESUS CHRIST for performance. AMEN.

DAY THREE (3)

PRAYING SCRIPTURE

1 CORINTHIANS 9:7, 9

"Who goeth a warfare any time at his own charges? who planteth a vineyard, and eateth not of the fruit thereof? or who feedeth a flock, and eateth not of the milk of the flock?

For it is written in the law of Moses, Thou shalt not muzzle the mouth of the ox that treadeth out the corn. Doth God take care for oxen?"

PRAY NOW

I DECREE & DECLARE

Dear Heavenly Father ,

I bless YOU for choosing me to be among YOUR beloved and according to YOUR divine purpose.

YOU are the author of purpose. Jeremiah was afraid to carry out YOUR divine plan, YOU gave him YOUR words and boldness; LORD supply everything I need to fulfil my purpose on this earth in the MIGHTY NAME OF JESUS.

David needed to confront Goliath, YOU gave him the Living Stone and YOUR presence. FATHER LORD, supply me with the tools of operations (YOUR presence, courage, money and destiny helpers) for my success, breakthroughs, victories and purpose for existence to be fully established in JESUS NAME.

I decree and declare that I shall eat and enjoy the proceeds of my labour. I will fight a good fight and my work, ministry and calling shall not suffer casualties in JESUS NAME.

I declare by the authority of YOUR words that my fulfilment, satisfaction and joy shall not be muzzled, my hope for living shall not be dashed and YOUR expectations for me to have a good future and an expected end shall come to pass in the MIGHTY NAME OF JESUS.

Life is full of wars and challenges, but just like YOU Partner with Moses, Joshua and David and they came out not as losers, victims or failures, let YOUR presence show up and partner with me in my present situations in JESUS NAME.

I declare boldly that my going out and coming in today is blessed and preserved in JESUS NAME.

I cover these prayers with the PRECIOUS BLOOD OF THE LORD JESUS CHRIST for performance. AMEN.

DAY FOUR (4)

PRAYING SCRIPTURE

EXODUS 32:1

"And when the people saw that Moses delayed to come down out of the mount, the people gathered themselves together unto Aaron, and said unto him, Up, make us gods, which shall go before us; for as for this Moses, the man that brought us up out of the land of Egypt, we wot not what is become of him."

PRAY NOW

I DECREE & DECLARE

Dear Heavenly Father,

Thank YOU for another beautiful day and a brand-new week YOU have given me.

By the power of YOUR HOLY SPIRIT at work in me, I shall have no occasion to turn aside to another GOD for any reason no matter how pressing or strong it may be in the NAME OF JESUS.

By the BLOOD OF JESUS, I decree and declare that every spirit of delay operating in my life today be scattered and utterly destroyed in the MIGHTY NAME OF JESUS.

O VOICE OF GOD, release thunder from heaven and let the foundation of delay and the power behind it in my life, family, finances, business, ministry, career, education, destiny, marriage, child bearing and fulfilment of purpose collapse in JESUS NAME.

Every delayed expectation in my life, I command you to receive divine speed from this moment and this very year in the MIGHTY NAME OF JESUS.

By YOUR MERCY O LORD, let oil of favour, speed and promotion in all my engagements and desires locate me in the MIGHTY NAME OF JESUS.

I decree that no project will suffer delay any longer in my hands in JESUS NAME.

By faith I receive Your divine allocation of my daily benefits today with gratitude in JESUS NAME.

I declare boldly that my going out and my coming in today is blessed in JESUS NAME.

I cover these prayers with the PRECIOUS BLOOD OF THE LORD JESUS CHRIST for performance. AMEN.

DAY FIVE (5)

PRAYING SCRIPTURE

1 TIMOTHY 1:18

"This charge I commit unto thee, son Timothy, according to the prophecies which went before on thee, that thou by them mightest war a good warfare;"

PRAY NOW

I DECREE & DECLARE

Dear Heavenly Father,

Now unto the KING ETERNAL, IMMORTAL, INVISIBLE, THE ONLY WISE GOD, be honour and glory forever and ever. AMEN

FATHER LORD, am not unaware that my weapon of warfare are not carnal but mighty. I therefore approach the remaining part of this week ahead, pulling down both visible and invisible strongholds in my journey and affairs in JESUS MIGHTY NAME.

I cast down all imaginations and all high things exalting or planning to exalt themselves against the plan and purpose of GOD in my life and family by THE PRECIOUS BLOOD OF JESUS CHRIST.

I bring every negative thought of evil (failure and death) against me, my family, finances, business, health, my spiritual life and general welfare into subjection and captivity by the authority of the Word of God and godly prophetic utterances that have gone before me in the NAME OF JESUS.

MIGHTY MAN IN BATTLE, I command and decree that every storm, every contrary situation on my path this year shall give way for my passage by force and by fire in the MIGHTY NAME OF JESUS.

I declare that every physical, emotional and spiritual mountain shall be subdued, every crooked way shall be made smooth and every Valley shall become level and even for my passage in the NAME OF JESUS.

I receive the grace to be obedient to YOUR words and directives. I command my spiritual eyes and ears to be opened. I receive the power of discernment and sensitivity. I shall not fall a victim of any battle in the NAME OF JESUS.

I receive YOUR daily loads of my benefits by faith today in JESUS NAME.

I decree and declare that my going out and coming in today is blessed and preserved in JESUS NAME.

I cover these prayers with the PRECIOUS BLOOD OF THE LORD JESUS CHRIST for performance. AMEN.

DAY SIX (6)

PRAYING SCRIPTURE

PHILIPPIANS 1:4-6

"Always in every prayer of mine for you all making request with joy,

For your fellowship in the gospel from the first day until now;

Being confident of this very thing, that he which hath begun a good work in you will perform it until the day of Jesus Christ"

PRAY NOW

I DECREE & DECLARE

Dear Heavenly Father,

I thank YOU for another day which YOU have made specifically and specially for me. I choose to rejoice and be glad in it.

I decree and declare that this is my Season of perfected testimonies in JESUS NAME

I declare, for every evil calculation and agenda from the pit of hell targeted at me and family GOD shall raise a Standard against them, and they shall go back to their senders in JESUS NAME.

I decree and declare that in my life, home and work there shall be speedy manifestation of GOD'S Counsels in JESUS NAME.

I receive into my life perfect physical, spiritual and material prosperity and sound health in JESUS NAME.

I decree and declare that I shall finish all my projects without suffering any delay any longer in JESUS NAME.

Today, I shall have testimonies on those long-awaited perfections in my destiny in JESUS NAME.

With outstretched hands I receive YOUR divine allocation of my daily benefits today with faith in JESUS NAME

I declare that my going out and coming in today is blessed and preserved in JESUS NAME. I cover these prayers with the PRECIOUS BLOOD OF THE LORD JESUS CHRIST for performance. AMEN.

DAY SEVEN (7)

PRAYING SCRIPTURE

GENESIS 29:31

"And when the LORD saw that Leah was hated, he opened her womb: but Rachel was barren."

PRAY NOW

I DECREE & DECLARE

Dear Heavenly Father,

Thank YOU for granting me life. Thank YOU for bringing me to the end of this month and preparation for another beautiful month. It is of YOUR MERCIES am not consumed.

FATHER LORD, according to Your word and its authority, I decree today and request by YOUR MERCY, let everything the devil, wicked people and demonic agents have closed down or planning to close down in my life and destiny be reopened with the new month within the next few hours in the MIGHTY NAME OF JESUS.

MY FATHER MY FATHER, let every embargo and limitations placed on my promotion, breakthroughs, business, joy in my family, finances and destiny be shattered in JESUS NAME.

LORD, BY YOUR MERCY and to the shame of my adversaries make a way for me where they have used their mortal power and influence to block me in JESUS NAME.

LORD, I open my hands to YOU, let my divine allocation of YOUR blessings come to me today and for the rest of this week in JESUS NAME.

I decree and declare that my going out and coming in today is blessed and preserved in JESUS NAME.

I cover these prayers with the PRECIOUS BLOOD OF THE LORD JESUS CHRIST for performance. AMEN.

DAY EIGHT (8)

PRAYING SCRIPTURE

EZEKIEL 47:12

"And by the river upon the bank thereof, on this side and on that side, shall grow all trees for meat, whose leaf shall not fade, neither shall the fruit thereof be consumed: it shall bring forth new fruit according to his months, because their waters they issued out of the sanctuary: and the fruit thereof shall be for meat, and the leaf thereof for medicine."

PRAY NOW

I DECREE & DECLARE

Dear Heavenly Father,

I thank YOU for a successful May and for ushering me into the new month of June.

I decree and pray that by YOUR MERCY this brand-new month, GOD will take me to my land of breakthrough.

I lay hold of all the provisions GOD has packaged into this month, my life and Destiny shall flourish, my health shall be at the top shape and divine supplies will attend to me in JESUS NAME.

I declare that all the powers and personalities that say my glory and destiny will not come to fruition and manifestation, GOD in His anger will send them to battle of no return this month in the MIGHTY NAME OF JESUS.

I decree and declare, GOD will enthrone me over and above my enemies, all those living like kings and dictators over my life are dethroned in JESUS NAME.

Any authority in the physical and the spiritual that wants to limit me shall be limited and cut down in JESUS NAME.

Everyone that shall go or is going from mountain to mountain, from prophets to prophets, from Alfas to sheiks, from witch doctors to herbalists for my downfall shall fall flat before me this month in the NAME OF JESUS.

This brand-new month, THE LORD GOD, will turn my tragedies into triumphs. GOD will turn my setback to comebacks and my disappointment to destiny appointments in the NAME OF JESUS.

This new month I declare that God will frustrate every Satanic plans against my Family, Career, Business, Marriage and Spiritual Life in the MIGHTY NAME OF JESUS.

I pray, GOD will perfect that which concerns me financially, spiritually and make me a blessing this month in JESUS MIGHTY NAME.

By faith, I receive YOUR divine allocations of my daily benefits today for my satisfaction in JESUS NAME

I declare that my going out and my coming in today is blessed and preserved in JESUS NAME. I cover these prayers with the PRECIOUS BLOOD OF THE LORD JESUS CHRIST for performance. AMEN.

DAY NINE (9)

PRAYING SCRIPTURE

EZRA 6:14-15

"And the elders of the Jews builded, and they PROSPERED through the PROPHESYING of Haggai the prophet and Zechariah the son of Iddo. And they BUILDED, and FINISHED it, according to the commandment of the God of Israel, and according to the commandment of Cyrus, and Darius, and Artaxerxes king of Persia.

And this house was finished on the third day of the month Adar... "

PRAY NOW

I DECREE & DECLARE

Dear Heavenly Father,

Thank YOU again for your love, protection and life given to them that are with me in this platform and contact point all over the world in JESUS NAME.

Operating from the office of the Prophet this great day, I decree and declare over you that What you could not do before now shall receive divine attention and intervention from the above for speedy take off and completion in JESUS NAME.

I decree and declare that any force that has been hindering you from building your destiny, YOUR family, YOUR finances, YOUR business, YOUR work, YOUR health, YOUR purpose, YOUR dreams and YOUR peace, let that force be dis-empowered and catch fire in this new month the MIGHTY NAME

OF JESUS.

All the hired counsellors against you to frustrate your purpose and journey of life shall be disappointed after the order of Balaam and Haman in the NAME OF JESUS.

Any document written against you or intended to be written against you shall be reversed this month in JESUS NAME.

Anything that has ceased flowing meant for your enjoyment, joy and peace shall be re-opened this month with greater force in JESUS NAME.

Every day of this month you shall see the token of GOD's goodness and HIS mighty Hands upon your life and destiny in JESUS NAME.

From today to the end of this month, it shall be from one positive divine helps and encounter to another.

It is the month that will refine and redefine your entire life, purpose and destiny in line with YOUR creation in the NAME OF JESUS

For your loss and what you were formally denied before now you shall be compensated and receive double in JESUS NAME.

You will enjoy Strange Opportunities and Divine Contacts and Connections in JESUS NAME.

Anyone plotting or planning your downfall will go down for you this month in JESUS NAME.

I declare boldly that your going out and coming in today and every day of this day shall be blessed abundantly and preserved jealously in THE MIGHTY NAME OF JESUS.

I cover these decrees and prayers with the precious blood of the LORD Jesus Christ for performance. AMEN.

REMEMBER TO SHARE YOUR TESTIMONY WITH ME BECAUSE SOMETHING GOOD WILL SOON HAPPEN IN YOUR LIFE.

DAY TEN (10)

PRAYING SCRIPTURE

JOB 22:28

"Thou shalt also decree a thing, and it shall be established unto thee: and the light shall shine upon thy ways."

PRAY NOW

DECREES & DECLARATIONS FROM ME TO YOU FOR THIS WEEK

Dear Heavenly Father,

THANK YOU FOR THE LIFE OF THIS YOUR CHILD.

I DECREE AND DECLARE THAT:

EVERY BARRIER BETWEEN YOU AND YOUR PROMISED LAND (OF GOOD JOB, FRUITFULNESS, PROSPERITY, BLISSFUL HOME, EXCELLENCE, GOOD RESULTS, BREAKTHROUGHS AND SPIRITUAL PROGRESS) IS DESTROYED TODAY IN JESUS MIGHTY NAME!

BECAUSE EVERY TREE MY HEAVENLY FATHER HAS NOT PLANTED SHALL BE ROOTED OUT, I DECREE THAT YOUR STRUGGLES ARE OVERTURNED FROM THEIR ROOTS TODAY IN JESUS NAME!

BECAUSE GOD SAYS THAT WHOSOEVER I BLESS SHALL BE BLESSED, I DECREE THAT YOU ARE COMING UNDER THE SHOWERS OF GOD'S BLESSINGS TODAY, THIS WEEKEND, THIS MONTH AND HENCEFORTH IN JESUS NAME.

THE DRY SEASONS OF YOUR LIFE ARE FINALLY OVER TODAY IN JESUS NAME.

FROM TODAY, BEGIN TO LIVE ABOVE OPPRESSION AND DEPRESSION IN JESUS NAME.

EVERY POWER PROLONGING YOUR JOURNEY FOR PERFORMANCE AND ACCOMPLISHMENTS IS CURSED TO DRY FROM THE ROOT IN JESUS NAME.

EVERY FORCE CHALLENGING YOUR HEALTHY LIVING IS SCATTERED AND DAMAGED ORGAN IN YOUR BODY IS RESTORED TO PERFECT STATE IN JESUS NAME.

EVERY FORM OF TERMINAL DISEASE UNDER THE SOUND OF THESE DECLARATIONS IS TERMINATED NOW IN THE NAME OF JESUS.

ALL CURRENT AND IMPENDING SHAME AND RIDICULES SHALL BE TURNED TO GLORY AND HONOUR IN JESUS NAME.

AGAIN, I DECREE, THAT SICKNESS AND DISEASE ARE ROOTED OUT OF YOUR BODY RIGHT NOW IN THE NAME OF JESUS!

EVERY FORCE CHALLENGING YOUR SPIRITUAL AUTHORITY IS BROUGHT UNDER YOUR CONTROL IN THE MIGHTY NAME OF JESUS.

RECEIVE THE BLESSINGS OF SUPERNATURAL BREAKTHROUGHS IN JESUS NAME.

YOUR MIRACLE MARRIAGE, JOB, BLESSINGS, AND MIRACLE CHILDREN BECOME YOURS RIGHT NOW IN JESUS NAME.

THAT YOUR PROJECT SHALL NOT BE ABANDONED IN JESUS NAME.

YOU ARE DELIVERED FROM MANIPULATIONS IN JESUS NAME.

THE NEW THINGS GOD IS DOING SHALL BEGIN WITH YOU IN THE MIGHTY NAME OF JESUS.

VERY SOON YOU SHALL ENJOY OPEN REWARDS FOR YOUR LABOURS AND STRUGGLES IN JESUS NAME!

BECAUSE THE SCRIPTURES SAY HE HAS NOT GIVEN US THE SPIRIT OF FEAR BUT OF LOVE, POWER AND SOUND MIND, I DECLARE THAT YOUR SOURCE OF FEAR IS TERMINATED. YOUR FEAR WILL TURN TO TESTIMONY AND MIRACLES IN JESUS NAME

ALL THESE DECLARATIONS PROCLAIMED ON YOUR LIFE WILL START MANIFESTING TODAY IN JESUS NAME!

YOUR GOING OUT AND COMING IN TODAY IS BLESSED AND PRESERVED IN JESUS NAME.

I COVER THESE DECREES AND DECLARATIONS WITH THE PRECIOUS BLOOD OF THE LORD JESUS CHRIST FOR PERFORMANCE. AMEN.

DAY ELEVEN (11)

PRAYING SCRIPTURE

ESTHER 6:1-4

"On that night could not the king sleep, and he commanded to bring the book of records of the chronicles; and they were read before the king.

And it was found written, that Mordecai had told of Bigthana and Teresh, two of the king's chamberlains, the keepers of the door, who sought to lay hand on the king Ahasuerus.

And the king said, What honour and dignity hath been done to Mordecai for this? Then said the king's servants that ministered unto him, There is nothing done for him.

And the king said, Who is in the court? Now Haman was come into the outward court of the king's house, to speak unto the king to hang Mordecai on the gallows that he had prepared for him....

verse 14" (Read Please)

PRAY NOW

I DECREE & DECLARE

Dear Heavenly Father,

I thank YOU for the blessing of another day and another week.

Let my book of remembrance be opened as you take stock of

the end of the second quarter of this year O LORD.

I decree and put an end to every and all ungodly postponement of my day of honour, goodness, joy, promotion, deliverance and celebration in JESUS NAME.

FATHER LORD, remember me; reward my past good deeds, my past prayers, fasting, faithfulness, tithings, labour, services, giving, holiness or indeed any good I have done over the years in the NAME OF MIGHTY JESUS.

The day Haman prepared death for Mordecai was the day GOD announced Mordecai's promotion; Father, turn every plan of my enemies against me to promotions & celebrations for the remaining part of this year in the name of Jesus.

I decree and declare that the beginning of my promotion, joy, honour and glory will mark the beginning of shame of my enemies in JESUS NAME.

I declare that the mouth my enemy is preparing to use to announce my misfortune or death shall be the megaphone that will be used to announce my undeniable and unstoppable testimony in JESUS NAME.

I decree that my helpers will lose their sleep this week because GOD will force them to remember me for good in JESUS NAME.

Mordecai was remembered at an unusual time of the day, Lord let me be remembered even when it does not look convenient or timely by my helpers and relevant authorities in JESUS NAME.

O LORD REMEMBER ME AND MY HOUSEHOLD FOR GOOD, WE SHALL NOT END THIS QUARTER OF THIS YEAR EMPTY IN JESUS NAME (7 TIMES)

I decree and declare that my going out and coming in today and throughout this week shall be blessed and preserved in JESUS NAME

I cover these prayers with the PRECIOUS BLOOD OF THE LORD

JESUS CHRIST for performance. AMEN.

DAY TWELVE (12)

PRAYING SCRIPTURE

ISAIAH 28:18

"And your covenant with death shall be disannulled, and your agreement with hell shall not stand;..."

ISAIAH 54:10.

"For the mountains shall depart, and the hills be removed; but my kindness shall not depart from thee, neither shall the covenant of my peace be removed, saith the LORD that hath mercy on thee."

PRAY NOW

I DECREE & DECLARE

Dear Heavenly Father,

I give YOU thanks for YOUR tender mercy, kindness and YOUR covenant of peace that have kept me since the year began till now.

By the power of YOUR covenant I decree and declare that every satanic agreement of certain personalities, authorities or people over me is scattered in JESUS NAME.

O storm of sickness and death, you shall not prevail over me in JESUS NAME.

I decree and break every covenant of death or evil made by anyone living or dead over me and my loved ones by the BLOOD OF JESUS.

FATHER LORD, by YOUR MERCY and covenant of peace over

me, I declare that I shall live to fulfil destiny and divine plan in JESUS NAME.

I shall not sorrow over nor bury anyone belonging to me this year. I and the loved ones the LORD has given me shall live to fulfil the number of our days. No one of us shall die young in JESUS NAME.

By YOUR Hand of protection and preservation, preserve and lift me above those planning to bring me down and I declare that your kindness shall not depart from me in JESUS NAME.

By the BLOOD OF JESUS, I decree and declare that my going out and coming in today is blessed and preserved in JESUS NAME.

I cover these prayers with the precious blood of the LORD Jesus Christ for performance. AMEN.

DAY THIRTEEN (13)

PRAYING SCRIPTURE

JEREMIAH 51:20-26

"Thou art my battle axe and weapons of war: for with thee will I break in pieces the nations, and with thee will I destroy kingdoms;"

PRAY NOW

I DECREE & DECLARE

Dear Heavenly Father,

Thank YOU for one more day and for the weapons of our warfare, that are not carnal but mighty through YOU, to the pulling down of stronghold.

FATHER, in anyway, I have fallen short of your glory, have mercy and forgive me. Give me the grace to live above sin, and all the activities of the flesh in JESUS NAME.

By your mercy, please fight my battles and defend my cause.

Help me to put on Your whole armour, that I may be able to stand against wiles of the devil in the mighty name of Jesus.

Today, I take authority over demons, principalities, power, and spiritual wickedness, in high places, and I pull down their strongholds, in my life and destiny, in my home, family, finances, business, ministry and calling in JESUS NAME.

FATHER LORD, I declare my spirit, soul and body healthy. Let every satanic deposit, causing sickness and diseases, in my body, be destroyed and flushed out by the BLOOD OF JESUS.

I decree and declare that no weapon of sickness, poverty, lack, failure, unfruitfulness and death, fashioned against me shall Prosper in the MIGHTY NAME OF JESUS.

FATHER, let every expectation of my adversary and satanic bondage and limitation, in my life, catch fire and be destroyed completely in the MIGHTY NAME OF JESUS.

By Your grace, my victory shall be celebrated very shortly any time from today in JESUS NAME.

By faith, I receive Your divine allocation of my daily benefits today for my satisfaction in JESUS NAME.

By the BLOOD OF JESUS, I declare that my going out and my coming in today is blessed and preserved in JESUS NAME.

I cover these prayers with the PRECIOUS BLOOD OF THE LORD JESUS CHRIST for performance. AMEN

DAY FOURTEEN (14)

PRAYING SCRIPTURE:

1 PETER 5:10

"But the God of all grace, who hath called us unto his eternal glory by Christ Jesus, after that ye have suffered a while, make you perfect, stablish, strengthen, settle you."

HEBREWS 11:10

"For he looked for a city which hath foundations, whose builder and maker *is* God."

PRAY NOW

I DECREE AND DECLARE

Dear Heavenly Father,

Thank YOU for all things (life, protection, provision, good health)

YOU are the GOD of all grace, who called me to YOUR eternal glory by CHRIST JESUS.

By the authority of your word and love I declare and decree that I shall be made perfect in the areas am presently experiencing weakness and setback in JESUS NAME.

Today, I ride on prophetic word and the anointing of the HOLY SPIRIT that my destiny shall be restored and Established despite the situations surrounding me in JESUS NAME.

Strengthen my soul, body and spirit for greater exploits and settle me with undeniable results and terminate all my sufferings in JESUS NAME.

FATHER LORD, anoint me today with fresh oil. Let me experience the substance and see the evidence of the things that I have faith for - HEALING, BREAKTHROUGH, GLORY, FAVOUR, WEALTH, FREEDOM, SPIRITUAL UPLIFT-MENT and UNCOMMON BLESSINGs in JESUS NAME.

Like Abraham, I refuse to be weak in faith.

I declare that my body, soul and spirit are not dead but alive to birth out the purpose, gifts and anointing that God has set me aside for and set aside for me in JESUS NAME.

I receive all that GOD has promised me in full measure without losing any portion to the devil and the activities of his cohort around me in

I declare boldly that My going out and coming in today is blessed and preserved in JESUS NAME

I cover these prayers with the PRECIOUS BLOOD OF THE LORD JESUS CHRIST for performance. AMEN.

DAY FIFTEEN (15)

PRAYING SCRIPTURE

ECCLESIASTES 9:11-12

"I returned, and saw under the sun, that the race is not to the swift, nor the battle to the strong, neither yet bread to the wise, nor yet riches to men of understanding, nor yet favour to men of skill; but time and chance happeneth to them all.

For man also knoweth not his time: as the fishes that are taken in an evil net, and as the birds that are caught in the snare; so are the sons of men snared in an evil time, when it comes suddenly upon them."

PRAY NOW

I DECREE & DECLARE

Dear Heavenly Father,

After all my journey and adventures all over the face of the earth, I return this morning to say thank YOU for YOUR faithfulness and love for me.

Am not the swiftest, fastest or the smartest yet am on the winning side over sickness and death, over poverty and wretchedness, over spiritual barrenness and emptiness. This is the demonstration of YOUR love and Favour.

Many have given up and many have died this year but YOU have kept me. I just return today as YOUR grateful son (daughter) to say a big THANK YOU IN JESUS NAME.

The battle is not to the strong. Where the strongest people like giant Goliath has fallen in the battle of life this day, YOU are still fighting my battle like YOU did for the seemingly powerless David.

YOU made me to become a champion over my enemies where they were determined to have made me a prey and shred me by now.

I return today to say thank YOU for the undeserved victory YOU orchestrated for my triumph in Jesus NAME.

Many as wise as lion have suffered and died of hunger but YOU have kept supplying me with daily provisions and victuals according to YOUR riches in glory.

I return today and say thank YOU for your mercy that prevailed over me and my family in JESUS -.

YOU did not allow me and my family members be caught in an evil net nor permit the sons of men snare me in an evil time like this nor allow sudden death fall upon me.

FATHER, I just want to say thank YOU for supernatural protection despite all odds in JESUS NAME.

I decree and declare by YOUR MERCY that the flow of YOUR Favour and grace shall not cease in my life and family in JESUS NAME.

Thou shall PERFECT ALL THINGS concerning me and my family in the MIGHTY NAME OF JESUS.

By the BLOOD OF JESUS, I decree and declare that my going out and coming in today is blessed and preserved in JESUS NAME.

I cover these prayers with the PRECIOUS BLOOD OF THE LORD JESUS CHRIST for performance. AMEN.

DAY SIXTEEN (16)

PRAYING SCRIPTURE

JUDGES 8:4"And Gideon came to Jordan, and passed over, he, and the three hundred men that were with him, faint, yet pursuing them".

Isaiah 40:28-31 "Hast thou not known? hast thou not heard, that the everlasting God, the LORD, the Creator of the ends of the earth, fainteth not, neither is weary? He giveth power to the faint; and to them that have no might he increaseth strength."

PRAY NOW

I DECREE & DECLARE

Dear Heavenly Father,

I thank YOU because YOU are an everlasting FATHER who faints not nor become weary. YOU neither sleep nor slumber for my sake. I bless YOU today and for evermore for giving me power and strength to stay alive.

By YOUR MERCY O LORD, I decree and declare that I shall not be weary and I shall not faint because of any physical or spiritual Jordan of life or at every trouble spot and challenges am facing on this journey right now in JESUS NAME.

FATHER, by YOUR MERCY, I receive renewal of my inner and physical strength, health and mental prowess to deliver and receive the goods in JESUS NAME.

I receive the competence, skill, dexterity, proficiency, expertise and ability to stay on top of the game of life, to continue this race and finish excellently ahead of my competitors and other forces contending and challenging my purpose and existence in JESUS NAME.

I decree and declare that Nothing good that I have determined or purposed to do or achieve shall be abandoned or lack provision for execution in JESUS NAME.

FATHER LORD, turn my insufficiency to abundance and bless me with huge and never-ending provisions in JESUS NAME.

I shall mount up with wings as Eagles and ride above the tides and obstacles on my path to stardom, fulfilment and celebrations in the MIGHTY NAME OF JESUS.

With wide opened hands I receive my daily provisions and my today's benefits from YOU by faith in JESUS NAME.

By the BLOOD OF JESUS, I decree and declare that my going out and coming in today is blessed and preserved in JESUS NAME.

I cover these prayers with the PRECIOUS BLOOD OF THE LORD JESUS CHRIST for performance. AMEN.

DAY SEVENTEEN (17)

PRAYING SCRIPTURE

ROMANS 8:28

"And we know that all things work together for good to them that love God, to them who are the called according to his purpose".

1 JOHN 4:20

"If a man say, I love God, and hateth his brother, he is a liar: for he that loveth not his brother whom he hath seen, how can he love God whom he hath not seen?"

PRAY NOW

I DECREE & DECLARE

Dear Heavenly Father,

Thank YOU for YOU are the beginning and end of all things.

Thank YOU for giving me a brand-new beautiful weekend and preparing me for a new week that is going to be full of YOUR power and majesty in JESUS NAME.

My HEAVENLY FATHER, let YOUR love find expression in my heart and practically in my life.

Let YOUR love be shed aboard in my heart and towards humanity.

I receive the grace to abide by the golden rule, to do to others the way I would like them do to me and to treat them the way I would like to be treated in JESUS NAME.

I place demand on the authority of YOUR word and my calling

according to YOUR purpose;

I decree and declare that all things shall work together for my goodness this weekend and the new week about to be hatched and at all times in JESUS NAME.

FATHER LORD, let all my conscious and unconscious decisions, actions, inactions, words, deeds and movements this weekend, the week ahead and beyond work for my goodness, joy, breakthroughs, progress, and fulfilment where I desire and deserve them in the MIGHTY NAME OF JESUS.

Joseph committed error of telling his dreams to his brothers and led to the fulfilment of his glorious destiny and landed him in the palace. HOLY SPIRIT, let all my errors over the years move me and force me into the fulfilment of my divine purpose and destiny by the BLOOD OF JESUS.

The bitterness of Haman brought Mordecai from the position of a gateman to leadership with influence even in a foreign country. FATHER, let all the activities of my enemies towards me for the rest of this year lead to my miracle and promotion in JESUS NAME.

When Leah was hated, YOU opened her womb for conception and shocked her haters. FATHER LORD, by YOUR love for me, open up whatever the enemy has shut down in my life and turn every point at which am being hated to my joy and celebration in JESUS NAME.

By faith I receive my daily portion of YOUR benefits to enjoy and run my affairs today in JESUS NAME.

By the BLOOD OF JESUS, I declare that my going out and coming in today is blessed and preserved in JESUS NAME.

I cover these prayers with the PRECIOUS BLOOD OF THE LORD JESUS CHRIST for performance. AMEN

REMEMBER TO SHARE YOUR TESTIMONY WITH ME BECAUSE SOMETHING GOOD WILL SOON HAPPEN IN YOUR LIFE.

DAY EIGHTEEN (18)

PRAYING SCRIPTURE

1 TIMOTHY 6:12

"Fight the good fight of faith, lay hold on eternal life, whereunto thou art also called, and hast professed a good profession before many witnesses".

PRAY NOW

I DECREE & DECLARE

Dear Heavenly Father,

Thank YOU for qualifying me as a candidate for the fight of faith because a dead person doesn't contend with or for anything, thank YOU for the weapons of our warfare, that are not carnal but mighty through YOU, to the pulling down of stronghold.

FATHER, in anyway l have fallen short of your glory, by loosing faith in the authority and potency of Your word have mercy and forgive me in JESUS NAME.

I decree that my faith shall not fail me.

FATHER, increase my faith and give me the grace to live above sin, and all the activities of the flesh in the MIGHTY NAME OF JESUS.

FATHER LORD, please fight my battles that are weakening my spirit, soul and body and making me vulnerable. Defend my cause O LORD in the NAME OF JESUS.

FATHER LORD, I boldly put on YOUR total armours, and l declare my stand against wiles of the devil and their activities today in JESUS NAME.

I decree, declare and I take authority over demons, principalities, power, and spiritual wickedness, in high places, and by faith 1 pull down their strongholds and their effects in my life, destiny, ministry, home, family, spiritual life, finances my church and nation in the NAME OF JESUS.

By strong faith in YOU MY GOD, I declare and decree that every satanic deposit, causing sickness and diseases, in my body and inner being, be destroyed and flushed out by the BLOOD OF JESUS.

This new week, I decree and declare that every enchantment and divination against my success and breakthrough in life shall go back to the senders immediately in the NAME OF JESUS.

I decree that no weapon of sickness, poverty, lack, failure, and death, fashioned against me shall succeed nor prosper in JESUS NAME.

I prophesy that this week by the BLOOD OF JESUS that my going out and coming in every day is blessed and preserved in JESUS NAME.

I cover these prayers with the PRECIOUS BLOOD OF THE LORD JESUS CHRIST for performance. AMEN.

DAY NINETEEN (19)

PRAYING SCRIPTURE

JEREMIAH 29:11" For I know the thoughts that I think toward you, saith the LORD, thoughts of peace, and not of evil, to give you an expected end".

3 JOHN 1:2"Beloved, I wish above all things that thou mayest prosper and be in health, even as thy soul prospereth."

ISAIAH 14:27

"For the LORD of hosts hath purposed, and who shall disannul it? and his hand is stretched out, and who shall turn it back?"

PRAY NOW

I DECREE & DECLARE

Dear Heavenly Father, I thank YOU for YOUR banner of love over me. Thank YOU for keeping me alive by this hour of the day. Thank YOU for making my forehead stronger than that of my enemies. FATHER LORD, by the understanding of YOUR words, I made bold to declare that only YOUR counsel shall stand in my life. I curse every contrary imagination against me and my future in the MIGHTY NAME OF JESUS.

I decree and declare that the prosperity of my soul is un-negotiable, I shall be fat and flourishing spiritually beyond any contest from the pit of hell. I renounce and pull off any filthy garment the enemy has forced or trying to force on me by the BLOOD OF JESUS.

By YOUR MERCY, I remain a candidate to spend eternity with YOU. I shall not be distracted from the heavenly race and I shall not be a cast away from YOUR kingdom by the PRECIOUS BLOOD OF JESUS CHRIST.

Whatever the thief (devil) has stolen or destroyed in my body that may result to ill health I reclaim and recover it from this moment. I shall have life in abundance and not suffer breakdown in any of the organs of my body in the MIGHTY NAME OF JESUS.

Financial prosperity is my birth right and YOUR wish for me. Therefore, I decree with bold declaration that I shall not suffer scarcity of funds whenever I need it, I shall be great and not small. I remove my name from the vicious circle of reproaches, poverty, lack and wants. I declare the remaining part of the year 2017 a period of my unprecedented financial breakthroughs in JESUS NAME.

No evil is part of YOUR agenda for me. Therefore, my eyes shall see no evil, my family members shall suffer no evil occurrences this year in the MIGHTY NAME OF JESUS.

With faith and outstretched hands, I receive my divine allocations of YOUR daily benefits for me today in JESUS NAME.

I decree and declare that my going out and coming in today and this week is preserved and blessed in JESUS NAME.

I cover these prayers with the PRECIOUS BLOOD B OF THE LORD JESUS CHRIST for performance. AMEN.

DAY TWENTY (20)

PRAYING SCRIPTURE

ROMANS 8:26-27

"Likewise the Spirit also helpeth our infirmities: for we know not what we should pray for as we ought: but the Spirit itself maketh intercession for us with groanings which cannot be uttered.

And he that searcheth the hearts knoweth what is the mind of the Spirit, because he maketh intercession for the saints according to the will of God."

PRAY NOW

I DECREE & DECLARE

Dear Heavenly Father,

Thank YOU for another beautiful working day and for the ministry of the HOLY SPIRIT.

FATHER, I ask for the help of the HOLY SPIRIT today to stand in the gap and intercede on my behalf concerning the issues of my life.

LORD by the help of the HOLY SPIRIT, come and battle with everything I know or not known around me working against my life and destiny in the MIGHTY NAME OF JESUS.

Any power attempting to waste my destiny in any way or form, let them be wasted after the order of Pharaoh, Herod, Haman, and Saul in JESUS NAME.

By the help of the HOLY SPIRIT, I cancel whatever an expert has pronounced against me (doctor, lawyer, prophet, priest, enchanter, sheik, diviner, witch or wizard and…) in the MIGHTY NAME OF JESUS.

From today, and by the help of the Holy Spirit, let the Will of God be done in my life with accelerated speed in JESUS NAME.

By the help of the HOLY SPIRIT, I decree and declare that I shall maximize my potential and gifts. All my wasted years shall be converted to blessings in JESUS NAME.

By the help of the HOLY SPIRIT, I receive YOUR divine allocation of my daily benefits today in JESUS NAME.

I declare boldly that my going out and coming in today is blessed and preserved in JESUS NAME.

I cover these prayers with the PRECIOUS BLOOD OF THE LORD JESUS CHRIST for performance. AMEN.

DAY TWENTY-ONE (21)

PRAYING SCRIPTURE

PSALMS 25:1-2

"Unto thee, O LORD, do I lift up my soul.

O my God, I trust in thee: let me not be ashamed, let not mine enemies triumph over me".

PRAY NOW

I DECREE & DECLARE

Dear Heavenly Father,

Thank YOU for this great day that YOU have made. I will rejoice and be glad in it.

I have come today to refresh, re-establish and renew my allegiance to YOU.

Some trust in chariot and some trust in horses and some trust in other gods but this day, I make bold to renounce any other thing that may want to take YOUR place in my life and in my heart in the MIGHTY NAME OF JESUS.

Because I trust in YOU, I decree and declare that I shall not be ashamed over any issues of my life and the enemies shall not triumph nor have an occasion to laugh at me in JESUS NAME.

For any mess and embarrassment waiting, knocking my door and creeping into my life I receive double honour by faith this day. Let every force orchestrating disgrace and waiting for my shame be terminated and catch fire in JESUS NAME.

FATHER LORD, I decree and declare that every FINANCIAL SHAME and EMBARRASSMENTS in form of rents, accommodation, fees, bills, loan repayment, money to close a deal, to complete a project, to meet a deadline, to meet an obligation, to care for my family and my health, to secure a position of honour and dignity be terminated and receive divine supply in the MIGHTY NAME OF JESUS.

FATHER LORD, by YOUR MERCY, lead me in the truth and teach me the right way I should go. I shall no longer wander but shall become a wonder in this land in JESUS NAME.

By YOUR MERCY, remember not the sin of my youth and pardon my iniquity that might have caused me troubles and hardship in JESUS NAME.

By faith, I receive YOUR divine allocation of my daily benefits today in JESUS NAME.

By the BLOOD OF JESUS, I declare boldly that my going out and coming in today is blessed and preserved in JESUS NAME.

I cover these prayers with the PRECIOUS BLOOD OF THE LORD JESUS CHRIST for performance. AMEN.

DAY TWENTY-TWO (22)

PRAYING SCRIPTURE:

PROVERBS 25:28

"He that hath no rule over his own spirit is like a city that is broken down, and without walls."

PRAY NOW

I DECREE & DECLARE

Dear Heavenly Father,

Thank YOU for this beautiful day that YOU have made and I shall rejoice in it.

O you forces, influencing and pulling me back from growing spiritually I decree your destruction today in JESUS NAME.

I decree and declare that my wall of defence and protection shall not be broken. I shall not be exposed to the whims and caprice of the enemies in JESUS NAME.

By the BLOOD OF JESUS, I disorganize every spiritual altar / spirit set up to influence and manipulate me to act contrarily and negatively to the plan of GOD and HIS words in my life in the MIGHTY NAME OF JESUS.

I curse every power and force moving me against GOD'S expectation for my life; negative habits prevalent in my life and every spirit of error, I declare your destructions by the BLOOD OF THE LAMB today in JESUS NAME.

Every virtue broken down by the devil around me, I decree your reconstruction and restoration in the NAME OF JESUS.

HOLY SPIRIT, visit me and pour upon me the power of self-control over anger, excessive talking, malice, pride, lust of eyes and flesh, strife, Jealousy, selfishness, drunkenness, immorality, carousing, covetousness laziness, carelessness and lack of sense of accountability in the MIGHTY NAME OF JESUS.

I receive by the HOLY SPIRIT; joy, love, peace, patience, self-control, the spirit of holiness and power to be decisive into my life in JESUS NAME.

By the BLOOD OF JESUS, I decree and declare that my going out and coming in today is blessed and preserved in JESUS NAME.

I cover these prayers with the PRECIOUS BLOOD OF THE LORD JESUS CHRIST for performance. AMEN.

DAY TWENTY-THREE (23)

PRAYING SCRIPTURE

ROMANS 8:33

"Who shall lay anything to the charge of God's elect? It is God that justifieth".

PRAY NOW

I DECREE & DECLARE

Dear Heavenly Father,

I Thank YOU for another beautiful day that YOU have made for me to rejoice in the HOLY GHOST. And I thank YOU for counting me among the elects and beloved of Yours.

THANK YOU, FATHER, because by prophecy and YOUR confirmed words, this is still my year of divine increase, miracles, good reports and positive evidences of YOUR faithfulness in my life and family.

Today, I decree and declare that all powers, people and individuals that are also manufacturing or have devised evil and contrary evidences against me and fulfilment of your words and prophecy in my life to catch fire in the MIGHTY NAME OF JESUS.

FATHER LORD, by the power that silenced Pharaoh, Haman and Aithopel, come and lay to rest every force and their operators accusing me day and night both physically and spiritually in JESUS NAME.

I apply and plead the blood of Jesus to erase from their memories and files any negative evidence at their disposal about my past mistakes, errors, failures and the errors of my parents which they can use against me in the MIGHTY NAME OF JESUS.

Your words say, "who shall lay anything to the charge of GOD'S elect? It is GOD that justifies. By the authority of YOUR words I declare that no power can successfully accuse me this year. Either in my presence or behind me let the blood of Jesus show up any time my name is called for evil in JESUS MIGHTY NAME.

The allied forces of the angelic host shall confront every satanic accuser speaking evil evidences against my life, family, ministry, marriage, business, finances, job, career, and Destiny in JESUS NAME.

By faith, I receive my daily allocation of YOUR blessings into my life for me to run this day and weekend successfully in JESUS NAME.

By the BLOOD OF JESUS, I declare boldly that my going out and my coming in today is blessed and preserved in JESUS NAME

I cover these prayers with the PRECIOUS BLOOD OF THE LORD JESUS CHRIST for performance. AMEN.

DAY TWENTY-FOUR (24)

PRAYING SCRIPTURE

PHILIPPIANS 3:13

"Brethren, I count not myself to have apprehended: but this one thing I do, forgetting those things which are behind, and reaching forth unto those things which are before,"

ROMANS 8:18-19

"For I reckon that the sufferings of this present time are not worthy to be compared with the glory which shall be revealed in us.For the earnest expectation of the creature waiteth for the manifestation of the sons of God."

PRAY NOW

I DECREE & DECLARE

Dear Heavenly Father, I thank YOU for the bright new day and for YOUR daily helps. I thank YOU for giving me hope because to him that is joined with the living there is hope. I look unto JESUS today, the author and finisher of my faith, who for the joy set before him endured the cross and despised the shame. Therefore, I choose to forget the pains, sorrows, hardship and distractions I have ever suffered in my lifetime and look forward to the glory of the rest of my life with high expectations of greater achievements in JESUS NAME.

I refuse to grow weary or be discouraged because where am going is greater, better and bigger than where am coming from and my future will deliver into my life; joy, peace, goodness, prosperity, love, divine health, breakthroughs, fruitfulness, opportunities, advancement, rest round about and spiritual empowerment in JESUS NAME.

I decree and declare that whatever I could not achieve in the past shall become my testimonies before the end of this year in JESUS NAME.

I receive the grace to let go people that offended me because offence must come but woe to him by which it comes. I drop every unforgiving spirit that has the power to hinder the answer to my prayers in JESUS NAME.

From today, I choose by the GRACE OF GOD to forget every disappointment, betrayals, hurts, accusations and wrongs judgement passed on me ignorantly or deliberately in JESUS NAME.

I declare that my dreams shall become realities and every dreams killer shall be confused, disappointed and pained over my divine results. I receive divine connections and supports into my life in the NAME OF JESUS. Because the whole creatures are waiting for my manifestations, I shall not be a disappointment to my world but be a greater blessing in JESUS NAME.

The GLORY OF GOD shall manifest in my life and family without measures and my detractors would be forced to celebrate with me in JESUS NAME.

I decree and declare that my going out and coming in today is blessed and preserved in JESUS NAME.

I cover these prayers with the PRECIOUS BLOOD OF THE LORD JESUS CHRIST for performance. AMEN.

REMEMBER TO SHARE YOUR TESTIMONY WITH ME BECAUSE SOMETHING GOOD WILL SOON HAPPEN IN YOUR LIFE.

DAY TWENTY-FIVE (25)

PRAYING SCRIPTURE

Zephaniah 3:17 "**The LORD thy God in the midst of thee** *is* **mighty; he will save, he will rejoice over thee with joy; he will rest in his love, he will joy over thee with singing.** **Zephaniah 3:18** **I will gather** *them that are* **sorrowful for the solemn assembly,** *who* **are of thee,** *to whom* **the reproach of it** *was* **a burden.**

Zepheniah 3:19 Behold, at that time I will undo all that afflict thee: and I will save her that halteth, and gather her that was driven out; and I will get them praise and fame in every land where they have been put to shame.

Zephaniah 3:20 At that time will I bring you *again,* **even in the time that I gather you: for I will make you a name and a praise among all people of the earth, when I turn back your captivity before your eyes, saith the LORD.**

PRAY NOW

I DECREE & DECLARE

Dear Heavenly Father, I thank YOU and rejoice for this day. I slept and I woke up because you sustained me in my helpless night season. YOU are awesome and great is thy faithfulness. Morning by morning new mercies I see. I thank YOU for all I have needed Thy hand had provided.

FATHER LORD, turn my fear into testimony, joy and dancing moment in the NAME OF JESUS.

FATHER LORD, I know YOU are with me and YOU are mighty, by YOUR awesome, incontestable and unquestionable power save me from all open and secret oppressions, manipulations and whims of the satanic influences in JESUS NAME.

I decree and declare that from this faithful day every form of sorrow, reproach, accusation and criticisms around me and my family are terminated by the unwrinkled and unspotted BLOOD OF JESUS.

By the authenticity of YOUR word, undo all my afflictions, heal my wounds, my halts and I command these vices to be returned to the senders in manifold proportion in JESUS NAME.

I decree and declare that all my impending shame and in everywhere I have been put to shame shall turn to my fame and celebrations in the MIGHTY NAME OF JESUS.

By YOUR MERCY, restore my dignity and honour, and make me a name and a praise among my people, in this country and among all people of the earth in JESUS NAME.

By the BLOOD OF JESUS, I decree and boldly declare that my going out and coming in today is blessed and persevered in the NAME OF JESUS.

I cover these prayers with the PRECIOUS BLOOD OF THE LORD JESUS CHRIST for performance. AMEN

DAY TWENTY-SIX (26)

PRAYING SCRIPTURE

GENESIS 1:2-3, 5, 8, 13, 19, 23, 31

"And the earth was without form, and void; and darkness was upon the face of the deep. And the Spirit of God moved upon the face of the waters. And God said, Let there be light: and there was light. And God called the light Day, and the darkness he called Night. And the evening and the morning were the first day. And God called the firmament Heaven. And the evening and the morning were the second day. And the evening and the morning were the third day. And the evening and the morning were the fourth day. And the evening and the morning were the fifth day. And God saw everything that he had made, and, behold, it was very good. And the evening and the morning were the sixth day"

PRAY NOW

I DECREE & DECLARE

Dear Heavenly Father, Thank YOU for the work of creation and for creating me in your pleasure. Out of nothing by YOUR SPIRIT, power and awesomeness you created the heaven and earth: let YOUR HOLY SPIRIT saturate my life for new and amazing things to begin to emerge from my life in JESUS NAME.

By the forces of YOUR creative words let everything condemned, outdated and not working well in my life receive YOUR fresh breath and come alive in the MIGHTY NAME OF JESUS.

The summary of YOUR handiwork throughout the six days was the separation of light and darkness. Therefore, I decree and declare my separation from all the activities of the devil and the wicked ones around me and my family. I command them to catch fire by the HOLY GHOST IN JESUS NAME.

Weeping may endure for a night but joy cometh in the morning. FATHER, by the BLOOD OF JESUS, let every source of my weeping or that may cause me to weep wither off. Let my weeping turn to celebration and laughter before this year ends in JESUS NAME.

FATHER LORD, it took you six days to create all things and you rested on the seventh day; by YOUR favour, mercy and my faith in YOU, I receive rest concerning my present situation, my family, my marital affairs, finances, business, health and destiny in JESUS NAME.

Everything You did was within seven days, my HEAVENLY FATHER I believe you within the next 7 days for miracles, breakthroughs, opportunities, spiritual encounters, favours, blessings, breakthroughs, pleasant surprises, special gifts, good news, victory over my battles, open doors, and divine helps in the MIGHTY NAME OF JESUS.

I decree and declare that my going out and coming in today is blessed and preserved in JESUS NAME.

I cover these prayers with the PRECIOUS BLOOD OF THE LORD JESUS CHRIST for performance. AMEN.

BIRTHDAY PRAYERS

DEDICATED TO ALL THE JUNE BORN

(Celebrate with me, I was born today, June 27TH)

PRAYING SCRIPTURE

PSALMS 90:12

"So teach us to number our days, that we may apply our hearts unto wisdom."

PRAYERS FOR YOU

I DECREE & DECLARE

Dear Heavenly Father,

Thank YOU for the life of this YOUR child born sometimes ago in the month of June.

I Thank GOD for sustainability of your life and for adding to you a new year and a fresh start of life in JESUS NAME.

The good LORD will teach you how to number your days and how to apply your heart to wisdom which is the principal thing in the journey of life in JESUS NAME.

In this your new year, you shall receive into your life wisdom, which is the custodian of long life, riches, honour, strength, power, glory, and blessings in JESUS NAME.

According to DEUTERONOMY 11:21, your days shall be multiplied as the days of heaven upon the earth in JESUS NAME.

I decree and declare that your days and years shall be prolonged; and you shall not die before your heavenly bound and ordained number of years in the MIGHTY NAME OF JESUS.

Like David in (1 CHRONICLES 29:28), you shall arrive at a good old age, full of days, riches, and honour: and you will reign on earth in JESUS NAME.

By the authority of the word of GOD according to (PSALMS 72:7), in your days you shall flourish; and full of the abundance of peace so long as the moon endures in the MIGHTY NAME OF JESUS.

In this your new year, GOD will satisfy you early with His mercy and favour; that you may rejoice and be glad in all your days in JESUS NAME.

Because the bible says in ECCLESIASTES 5:18, "it is good and comely for one to eat and to drink, and to enjoy the good of all his labour that he takes under the sun all the days of his life, which God gave him: for his portion;

I declare boldly that you shall spend the rest of your days and years in pleasure in the NAME OF JESUS.

By power of the HOLY SPIRIT, I decree that problems and challenges that will make the elder to serve the younger never happen in your life In JESUS NAME.

I decree that, the rod of the wicked shall not rest upon you in JESUS NAME.

By the authority of GOD'S words, I decree and declare that in your new year you shall no longer witness:

Anxiety, breaking down, Borrowing & begging, Disappointment, Diseases, Lack and want, Failure of any kind, Frustration, Fruitlessness, Fear and faithlessness, Barrenness, Depression, Indebtedness, Joblessness, Losses, loneliness, Mockery and shame in the MIGHTY NAME OF JESUS.

In this new year of yours,

l Pray for your divine visitations, your new season shall bring to you; uncommon blessings, connections to your benefactors/partners, transformation,restoration and elevation.

Global doors of breakthrough unlimited shall open to you this year. You shall enjoy Divine Direction and Decisions. Your purpose shall be finally established this year. You will go higher and enjoy promotions this year. It shall be your year of unstoppable celebrations and victories round about in the MIGHTY NAME OF JESUS.

By the anointing of the HOLY SPIRIT, you shall become an "ETERNAL EXCELLENCY" in wheresoever men have written you off and have closed the case. I decree that, from now onward, good things shall come out of your Nazareth in JESUS NAME.

Through the greatness of GOD'S Power, you shall be made a spectator of your own battles as GOD takes over the known and unknown battles targeted to humiliate you. Henceforth, every Egyptian that you saw last year, you shall see them no more in JESUS NAME.

By the power of the HOLY SPIRIT, your generation after you shall be exempted from the consequences of the wrong and errors of your parents. Henceforth, GOD'S MERCY will clear all their mess as God makes His favour to speak for you in JESUS NAME.

By the blood of everlasting covenant, you shall never venture into anything that will make GOD to forsake you.

I decree that, from today onward, you shall only be involved in things that are right, just, holy, pure and of good reports in JESUS NAME.

Please say after me with faith:

"In this new year of mine.

I shall not beg to eat.

I shall not be ashamed.

I shall not be cursed.

I shall not cry over loved ones.

I shall not be mocked.

I shall not be a victim of hired killers.

I shall not be a victim of accidents.

I shall not be sorrowful in Jesus name.

I shall be great.

I shall be fruitful.

I shall be victorious.

I shall be celebrated.

I shall be successful.

I shall be favoured.

I shall be blessed in abundance.

I shall be prosperous.

I shall have joy unspeakable.

I shall have peace beyond limits.

I shall make it.

I shall testify to the glory of GOD.

I shall be lifted high beyond falling.

I shall excel in all that I do.

I shall be called Wonderful.

Where the road is thirsty of flesh and blood, I and my loved ones will not go there. This year, the evils that will happen will not know my dwelling place.

The miracles in the year shall locate me and my household.

My heart desires and expectations will not be cut off.

I will not cry this year in the MIGHTY NAME OF JESUS."

I cover these prayers with the PRECIOUS BLOOD OF THE LORD JESUS CHRIST for performance. AMEN

REMEMBER TO SHARE YOUR TESTIMONY WITH ME BECAUSE SOMETHING GOOD WILL SOON HAPPEN IN YOUR LIFE.

DAY TWENTY-EIGHT (28)

PRAYING SCRIPTURE

ROMANS 5:8

"But God commendeth his love toward us, in that, while we were yet sinners, Christ died for us."

2 CORINTHIANS 8:9

"For ye know the grace of our Lord Jesus Christ, that, though he was rich, yet for your sakes he became poor, that ye through his poverty might be rich."

PRAY NOW

I DECREE & DECLARE

Dear Heavenly Father, I woke up this morning with the attitude of gratitude and thanksgiving looking back at all YOU have done for me. FATHER, I thank YOU for not holding back YOUR only begotten son for my sake. YOUR SON, JESUS CHRIST is the reason for my life and existence for He completely took it upon HIMSELF all my troubles and woes. Am grateful O LORD.

HE was buffeted and punished for my sins and iniquity, JESUS, once more I have come to say thank YOU LORD.

The wages of sin is death but JESUS died for my sin so that I might live. Therefore, I decree and declare that the power and pang of sin has no effect over me by the BLOOD OF JESUS

CHRIST.

I decree and declare that sickness of any kind or form had no portion in my life again by the BLOOD OF JESUS.

I decree and declare that my bones and any part of my body shall not be broken by the devil because JESUS CHRIST already took my place for that, in JESUS NAME.

I decree and declare that lack and want is not my portion because Jesus already took my poverty away in JESUS NAME.

By the BLOOD OF JESUS, I terminate hardship and all the works of the devil around me because Satan has no legal right over my life in JESUS NAME.

I declare to the hearing and confusion of my enemies that am wet and soaked by the BLOOD OF JESUS today and my enemies are helpless concerning me and all that belong to me in JESUS NAME.

By the token of the blood, the destructive angel could not kill anyone in the camp of Israel; I decree and declare by the unspotted BLOOD OF JESUS, that I shall not die but live to declare the glory of GOD in my life in

JESUS NAME.

JESUS was never confused over any matter because HE said, "AM THE WAY," and He always knew what to do. I therefore declare and decree that I shall no longer be confused over any issue of my life and for the existing confusion if there is any, I receive divine direction today in the MIGHTY NAME OF JESUS.

I decree and declare that my going out and coming in today is blessed and preserved in JESUS NAME

I cover these prayers with the PRECIOUS BLOOD OF THE LORD JESUS CHRIST for performance. AMEN

DAY TWENTY-NINE (29)

PRAYING SCRIPTURE

1 TIMOTHY 1:18

"This charge I commit unto thee, son Timothy, according to the prophecies which went before on thee, that thou by them mightest war a good warfare;"

PRAY NOW

I DECREE & DECLARE

Dear Heavenly Father, Now unto the KING eternal, immortal, invisible, the only wise God, be honour and glory forever and ever. AMEN

FATHER LORD, am not unaware that my weapon of warfare are not carnal but mighty. I therefore approach the rest of this week pulling down both visible and invisible strongholds in my journey and affairs in JESUS MIGHTY NAME.

I cast down every imagination and every high thing exalting or planning to exalt themselves against the plan and purpose of GOD in my life and family this year by the PRECIOUS BLOOD OF JESUS CHRIST.

I bring every negative thought of evil (failure and death) against me, my family, finances, business, health, my spiritual life and general welfare into subjection and captivity by the authority of the WORD OF GOD and godly prophetic utterances that have gone before me in the NAME OF JESUS.

MIGHTY MAN IN BATTLE, I command and decree that every open and secret storms, spiritual roadblocks, mountains and valleys, hyenas, scorpions and pythons, giants, emotional instability, crookedness and every contrary situation on my path right now must give way for my passage by force; I call down fire on them in the MIGHTY NAME OF JESUS.

I receive the grace to be obedient to YOUR words and directives. I command my spiritual eyes and ears to be opened. I receive the power of discernment and sensitivity. I shall not fall a victim of any battle in the NAME OF JESUS.

I receive YOUR daily loads of my benefits into my life by faith today in JESUS NAME.

I decree and declare that my going out and coming in today is blessed and preserved in JESUS NAME.

I cover these prayers with the PRECIOUS BLOOD OF THE LORD JESUS CHRIST for performance. AMEN.

TODAY'S PROPHECY

THUS SAITH THE LORD:

"THIS YEAR IS NEVER LATE FOR ME TO MAKE YOUR DREAMS AND DESIRES COME TO PASS BETWEEN YOU AND THE FLESH YOUR FLESH AND BONES OF YOUR BONES."

DAY THIRTY (30)

PRAYING SCRIPTURE:

ISAIAH 52:1-2

"Awake, awake; put on thy strength, O Zion; put on thy beautiful garments... for henceforth there shall no more come into thee the uncircumcised and the unclean.

Shake thyself from the dust; arise, and sit down... loose thyself from the bands of thy neck, O captive daughter of Zion."

PRAY NOW

I DECREE & DECLARE

Dear Heavenly Father,

Thank YOU for waking me up. Thank YOU for watching over me in the night season and for me not to sleep the sleep of death.

By the word of YOUR power, I refuse and rebuke every regulating powers trying to keep me in the dust and positions where I don't belong. I decree that every curse of retrogression directed against me by any force be nullified. I and what GOD has blessed me with shall not go down in JESUS NAME.

FATHER LORD, deliver me from any form of mockery and ridicule hanging over my calling, finances, career, business, assignment, profession, family and my life in JESUS NAME.

I decree and declare that every power trying to abort my joy and happiness; forces striving to change my glorious destiny into pain, be destroyed in the NAME OF JESUS.

I loose myself from all forms of manipulations working against me. I loose myself by the BLOOD OF JESUS from every incantation, enchantment, evil proclamations and satanic declarations in JESUS NAME.

By YOUR MERCY O LORD, I reclaim my lost ground, I reclaim my divine position and destiny; I reclaim my lost glory, honour, power, wisdom, strength, riches and blessings in JESUS NAME.

By faith I receive YOUR divine allocation of my daily benefits today with an outstretched hand in JESUS NAME.

I decree and declare that my going out and coming in today is blessed and preserved in JESUS NAME.

I cover these prayers with the PRECIOUS BLOOD OF THE LORD JESUS CHRIST for performance. AMEN

TODAY'S PROPHECY

THUS, SAITH THE LORD,

"I shall compensate you for what you lost or forcefully taken away from you with a more delightful and pleasing replacement"

TESTIMONIES

Please, kindly send your testimonies to:

Greatminds2016@gmail.com

        OR

Pastorwale2001@yahoo.com

2ND QUARTER ENDED

Get VOLUME 1c for the *NEXT* quarter

YOU SHALL BE BLESSED.

ABOUT THE AUTHOR

Wale-Rich Oladunjoye

He is a self motivated person, so he grew up accepting responsiblity for his life. He disengaged from public service to accept the call to Gospel Ministry in 1994. He was a vibrant pastor under the Living Faith Church Worldwide for several years. He planted the Kingdom Global Harvest Ministries in 2005. He became a pastor under the Good Tidings Bible Church in 2012 till date. He is the Provost of the Mighty Warriors Bible College under the above ministry and also the Superintendent of Branch Churches. He has a masters degree in Christian Counselling from the Christian Leadership University U.S.A. He is an author of many other books. He is a Nigerian resident.

BOOKS BY THIS AUTHOR

I Decree And Declare : Praying Scriptures

The PRAYING SCRIPTURES BOOK is to make prayer life enjoyable for you. Scriptures are picked to addresss various issues of life. it addresses specific issues that may be affecting you or your family with the intention of providing solutions for them. There is no doubt , if you consistently use this prayer book you will eventually know how to pray fervently and effectually.

Wealth Creation: Be Financially Educated

I wrote this book so that you can come out of the complaining crowd and become a peculiar person of substance, influence and power. This book is not just another piece on how to make quick money. It is about making prosperity a life style. If you desire to eradicate poverty read on. If you desire to create wealth for your family and your generation forever, then i still advice you read on. You are going to learn all time - tested and proven principles that will illuminate you and place you permanently on the part of unending wealth. As you you read i see God that changes season and situation changing your position positively as a result of the wisdom you will encounter in this book.

Printed in Great Britain
by Amazon